The Gault Case

Legal Rights for Young People

Thomas J. Billitteri

Landmark Supreme Court Cases

Enslow Publishers, Inc.

40 Industrial Road	PO Box 38
Box 398	Aldershot
Berkeley Heights, NJ 07922	Hants GU12 6BP
USA	UK

http://www.enslow.com

Library of Congress Cataloging-in-Publication Data

Billitteri, Thomas J.
   The Gault case : legal rights for young people / Thomas J.
Billitteri.
         p. cm. — (Landmark Supreme Court cases)
Includes bibliographical references and index.
Summary: Examines the 1967 Supreme Court case in which the Court
ruled that juvenile courts cannot deprive children of certain
rights guaranteed by the Constitution.
   ISBN 0-7660-1340-5
   1. Gault, Gerald Francis, 1949 or 1950—Trials, litigation,
etc.—Juvenile literature. 2. Juvenile justice, Administration
of—United States—Juvenile literature. 3. Due process of
law—United States—Juvenile literature. 4. Children—Legal
status, laws, etc.—United States—Juvenile literature.
[1. Gault, Gerald Francis, 1949 or 1950—Trials, litigation, etc.
2. Justice, Administration of. 3. Children's rights. 4. Due process
of law. 5. Juvenile courts.] I. Title. II. Series.
   KF228.G377 B55   2000
   345.73'081—dc21
                                                    00-008515

Printed in the United States of America

10 9 8 7 6 5 4 3 2

To Our Readers: We have done our best to make sure all Internet addresses in this book
were active and appropriate when we went to press. However, the author and the publisher
have no control over and assume no liability for the material available on those Internet
sites or on other Web sites they may link to. Any comments or suggestions can be sent by
e-mail to comments@enslow.com or to the address on the back cover.

Photo Credits: Blackstone-Shelburne N.Y., p. 63; Courtesy of the Arizona
Historical Society/Tucson, AHS # 1000, p. 13; Courtesy of Frank Lewis, pp. 37,
48; Courtesy of Norman Dorsen, p. 78; Fabian Bachrach, Collection of the
Supreme Court of the United States, p. 68; Franz Jantzen, Collection of the
Supreme Court of the United States, pp. 105, 111; Harris and Ewing, Collection
of the Supreme Court of the United States, pp. 70, 101; History and Archives
Division, Department of Library Archives and Public Records, Phoenix, Arizona,
p. 51; Library of Congress, p. 21; National Archives, pp. 19, 24, 33; National
Geographic Society, Collection of the Supreme Court of the United States, p. 65;
Robert S. Oakes, Collection of the Supreme Court of the United States, p. 108.

Cover Photo: CORBIS-Digital Stock

Contents

1

A Neighbor's Complaint

More than thirty years ago, in the dusty desert town of Globe, Arizona, a boy named Gerald Gault touched off a debate that still goes on today. Fifteen-year-old Gerald Francis Gault was alone in his family's home on Monday, June 8, 1964. At about 10 A.M., an officer from the Gila County sheriff's department came to take him into custody.[1]

The arrest came as a result of a complaint by Ora Cook, a neighbor of the Gaults. She said she had received an obscene phone call. There was no proof to indicate who had made the call or spoken the allegedly dirty words. Nonetheless, the sheriff's office arrested Gerald and a friend of his, Ronnie Lewis, who was also fifteen, and brought them to the juvenile detention home in Globe.

Gerald's arrest may have seemed harsh, given the circumstances. But he had already been in trouble with the authorities in Gila County twice before on charges that were never proven. Two years earlier, someone claimed that Gerald, then thirteen, had taken another boy's baseball glove and lied about it to the police. Gerald was never formally accused of stealing the glove, and no hearing ever took place before a judge.

A few months before Cook's complaint about the phone call, Gerald was charged with grand theft. Apparently Gerald had been with another boy who was accused of stealing a woman's wallet. Juvenile Court Judge Robert E. McGhee put Gerald on probation for six months. He also suggested that things could get worse for Gerald if he did not stay out of trouble.

With Ora Cook's complaint, Gerald was in trouble again. The Juvenile Code of Arizona—the state law governing the conduct of minors—defined a delinquent minor as a child who has violated a law, regulation or ordinance; cannot be controlled by his parent because he is "incorrigible [uncontrollable], wayward [stubborn] or habitually disobedient;" is regularly absent from school or home; or regularly conducts himself in ways that would "injure or endanger the morals or health of himself or others."[2] Being judged a delinquent minor could have serious consequences for Gerald, especially because he was already on probation.

Despite the seriousness of the situation, Gerald was unable to look to his parents for help that June morning when an officer from the sheriff's department came to arrest him. His father, Paul, was at work at the Grand Canyon, several hundred miles to the north. His mother, Marjorie, was at a baby-sitting job elsewhere in Globe. Neither parent knew anything about Ora Cook's charge. In fact, the officer did not even leave a note at the Gaults' home explaining where Gerald was going, or why.[3]

Arriving home that evening, Gerald's mother was surprised to find her son gone. He was usually good about being home on time. She started preparing dinner and asked her older son, Louis, to search for Gerald at Ronnie Lewis's home. Louis learned that Gerald was at the detention home. He returned and told his mother, and together they went to the detention facility that evening. Marjorie Gault met with Gerald. She also spoke with the home's superintendent, Charles D. Flagg, who was also the deputy probation officer of Gila County.

Flagg told Gerald's mother about the alleged obscene phone call. He also said the case would come up for a hearing the next day, June 9, before Judge

McGhee. But Gerald's mother never received anything in writing—no statement of why Gerald was in custody, no list of formal charges, no notice of the upcoming hearing, and no advisory that she had a right to hire a lawyer to help Gerald.

That night, Gerald remained in the detention home. Flagg questioned him about the alleged phone call. The next morning, he talked to Gerald again. Later, he also talked to Ronnie Lewis, to see if the boys' stories had changed.

Though he had no proof that Gerald had made the phone call or spoken any dirty words, Officer Flagg filed a petition with the juvenile court. In it, he declared Gerald "a delinquent minor" and asked the court for a hearing and for an order regarding his "care and custody"—words that suggested he could be taken away from his family and sent to live in a juvenile detention facility. As serious as the petition was, though, Flagg did not give Gerald or his parents a copy of it. In fact, the Gaults would not even find out that it existed until more than two months later.

At the June 9 hearing, Gerald, his mother, older brother, and two probation officers—Flagg and Henderson—went to Judge McGhee's chambers and sat down. The setting was very different from a typical courtroom for a case involving an adult accused of a crime. For example, no lawyers were present. There was no court reporter or stenographer present to record what was said and done at the hearing. No one took an oath to tell the truth. Gerald was unable to confront his accuser, Ora Cook. Judge McGhee had not asked her to be present, nor did he require Ronnie Lewis to be there. Basically, Gerald was on his own.

The hearing began, and soon Judge McGhee asked Gerald if he had made the phone call to Ora Cook. Gerald was not told he had the right to remain silent and not answer the question. However, Gerald did speak. But because no record was kept, there would be a disagreement later about what Gerald said. Gerald's mother remembered her son responding that he merely dialed Cook's phone, asked if it was such and such a number, told Cook that a friend wanted to talk to her, and then handed the phone to Ronnie Lewis. But Officer Flagg would later say that Gerald admitted to making the dirty comments. And Judge McGhee would testify that Gerald admitted to saying some obscene words.

During the hearing, Judge McGhee gave Gerald a pep talk, telling him he could make something of himself. Someone—either Gerald or his mother—asked the judge what would happen to Gerald next. Would he be sent away to the Fort Grant Industrial School, an institution for delinquent children about seventy miles away? As Gerald's mother would remember it later, the judge replied, "No, I will think it over. I want a couple days to think it over."

Gerald stayed at the detention home until the afternoon of June 11 or 12, when Officer Flagg drove Gerald to the house where his mother was baby-sitting and dropped Gerald off. Officer Flagg did not meet Gerald's mother.

When Marjorie Gault saw Gerald, she was relieved. She thought Judge McGhee had made his decision in Gerald's case and decided to let him go free. Later that same afternoon, Officer Flagg returned, and this time he handed Marjorie Gault a piece of paper. It was not an official document or notice, and it had no information about any charges against her son. It simply read:

	Mrs. Gault:	
	Judge McGhee has set Monday June 15, 1964 at 11:00 A.M. as the date and time for further hearings on Gerald's delinquency.	
	(signed) Flagg.	

When she read it, Marjorie Gault did not focus on the words "Gerald's delinquency" or why that was included in the note despite the fact that he had not been found guilty of anything. She simply thought Gerald was being asked to show up for another hearing because he might have to tell his story about what his friend Ronnie had done.[4]

Even so, Marjorie Gault still had doubts. On Saturday, June 13, she spoke to Globe's police chief, Rod Weinberg, who was also her landlord. She thought that perhaps Gerald needed a lawyer. Chief Weinberger said that would not be necessary. Judge McGhee was giving Gerald a year's probation. Assured by the chief's statement, Marjorie Gault went to the June 15 hearing with Gerald and her husband, who had come home from the Grand Canyon. Ronnie Lewis and his father were also present this time, as was Officer Flagg.

Ora Cook was not present, however. Gerald's mother asked Judge McGhee why the woman who had accused her son was not there. "I wanted Mrs. Cook present so she could see which boy that [had] done the talking, the dirty talking over the phone," Marjorie Gault would explain later.[5] Judge McGhee told her that Cook did not need to be there.

Without telling the Gaults, the probation office had filed a report on Gerald with the juvenile court that day, listing the charge against him as "lewd phone calls." According to the Arizona Criminal Code, someone who used "vulgar, abusive or obscene language" that a woman or child could hear was guilty of a misdemeanor.[6] A misdemeanor, an offense that is less serious than a felony, is usually punishable by a fine or by imprisonment somewhere other than in a penitentiary. As with the petition declaring Gerald a "delinquent minor," the Gaults would not know about the existence of this probation report for more than two months.

Similar to what happened at Gerald's first hearing, there was a disagreement in this second session with Judge McGhee as to what, exactly, Gerald did or did not say. Gerald's mother and Officer Flagg did not remember Gerald admitting to making any lewd remarks on the phone. Judge McGhee remembered Gerald admitting to some of the obscene remarks, though not the more serious ones. No other evidence was presented about Gerald using lewd language. Ronnie Lewis did not say that Gerald had made any of the obscene remarks to Ora Cook. And Cook was never asked to tell her story to the court.

Despite the lack of clear evidence against Gerald and the absence of any testimony against him from any adult, Judge McGhee ruled at the end of this second hearing that Gerald was indeed a "delinquent minor."

He said Gerald should be sent to the Fort Grant Industrial School for more than five years until he turned twenty-one.

According to Judge McGhee's order, Gerald's "own good and the best interests of the State require that he be committed."[7] Ironically, the Arizona Criminal Code said the punishment for making a lewd phone call was a five-dollar to a fifty-dollar fine or not more than two months in jail. But that punishment was for adults. Under the juvenile justice system, the judge could impose just about any sanction he thought was appropriate.

When Judge McGhee ruled that Gerald was a "delinquent minor," Gerald was sent to the Fort Grant Industrial School shown here.

After Judge McGhee's decision, a heart-wrenching scene occurred. Gerald's mother asked Judge McGhee if she could kiss Gerald goodbye. The judge refused.

Meanwhile, Gerald had asked for his Bible and some other personal belongings. Officer Flagg denied his request.

And so Gerald Gault, a fifteen-year-old boy who had never been convicted of a crime in a court, was being locked up in an institution far from home until he became an adult.

2

Foundations of Due Process

No State shall . . . deprive any person of life, liberty, or property, without due process of law; nor deny to any person within its jurisdiction the equal protection of the laws.[1]

Figuring out how to deal with children who are accused of crimes has always been difficult. Some young people commit horrible acts—even murder—and their cases are dealt with under the same criminal justice system that is used for adults. That often entails tough trial procedures and harsh punishment, including long prison sentences.

But experts warn that juveniles are not "little adults," and that in many cases—especially those involving less serious crimes—exposing young offenders to the adult criminal system is unfair. Still, young people should be held accountable for their actions. Some way must be found to determine their guilt or innocence. Then they must be put on the path to reform.

For centuries, lawmakers, judges, social activists, and legal experts have tried to think of ways to solve this problem. A century ago, a group of child advocates in Illinois thought they had the answer. They developed the juvenile court system. Their idea was simple: Juvenile courts would guide and rehabilitate young people who were accused of wrongdoing. Young offenders would not be given the same kind of severe punishment that would be handed out to adults. Special judges would hear juvenile cases in an informal setting and then rule according to each child's individual circumstances. Like a concerned parent, the judge would rule in a way that would help put the child back on the right track. Even when corrective action was necessary, it would be called "treatment," not "punishment," and it would take place in reform facilities, shelters, and trade schools, not prisons or penitentiaries.

After the juvenile courts were established, many adult legal protections no longer applied in juvenile cases. For example, the accused juvenile did not have the right to question the accusers under oath, or have the right to be tried before a jury of citizens. Supporters of the juvenile courts believed it would be easier to build trust and understanding if the environment was friendly, not confrontational.

The juvenile court system soon spread nationwide. It helped put many young people on a positive course. But there were problems. Because judges had so much flexibility, some of them decided that more discipline—not less—was best. They forgot about the *treatment* aspect of dealing with child offenders. Instead, they sent juveniles to workhouses and detention homes that were prisons in everything but name. In other cases, juveniles were accused of crimes they did not commit, and the juvenile court system gave them few opportunities to prove their innocence.

Thus, the juvenile justice system represented a compromise. While it sometimes protected young people from the harshness of the adult criminal system, it also took away many of the rights that protect adult citizens from government abuse.

To understand this trade-off in greater detail, it is necessary to learn about two legal traditions that play an important role in both our adult and juvenile systems of justice. One tradition is called *due process of law*. That term refers to a system of strict procedures and constitutional safeguards that ensures government authorities do not abuse their power when dealing with citizens. The system ensures that every accused person will have a day in court, and that each person's legal rights will be enforced. The other tradition is known as the doctrine of *parens patriae*. It is a Latin term that means the state—or government—is the ultimate parent and protector of every citizen. Where juvenile justice is concerned, *parens patriae* means that a court should treat a young offender the same way a wise and loving parent treats a disobedient child—not as a criminal, but as a person who needs understanding, guidance, protection, and, perhaps, rehabilitation.

Due Process Rights

From America's earliest days, an adult who was accused of a crime had the right to demand a fair trial. That tradition dates back to the Magna Carta, an English legal document that was issued in 1215. The Magna Carta, also known as the Great Charter, spelled out a number of personal liberties that were granted to free adults—those not living in servitude or slavery.

The Magna Carta declared that people could not be arrested or put in prison except through the "lawful" judgment of their peers and "by the law of the land." It also said that people deserved protection against the loss of life, liberty, or property, except in accordance with

The Magna Carta (shown here in its original Latin form) was an English document issued in 1215. It spelled out a number of personal liberties that were granted to free adults.

the law of the land. Such ideas came to form part of what we call *due process of law.*

The Magna Carta and its ideas about individual freedom were well-known to America's founding fathers in the late 1700s. The Magna Carta and other early English legal documents had a powerful influence on the thinking of early American leaders such as Thomas Jefferson, John Adams, and James Madison. But in drafting the United States Constitution, the founders did not focus as much on spelling out individual rights as they did on getting the new national—or federal—government off to a good start. Thus, the Constitution, put into effect in 1789, contained no list of personal liberties for the newly formed United States. As a result, many states feared that the federal government would have too much power over the private lives of citizens. Virginia and a number of other states demanded that the Bill of Rights—a list of individual freedoms, protections, and liberties—be added to the Constitution.

Madison, a member of the House of Representatives from Virginia and later the fourth president of the United States, led the effort to include the Bill of Rights. He looked to his own state's constitution, the Virginia Declaration of Rights, as a model. Virginia's constitution was based on the Magna Carta, on the

James Madison (shown here) was one of several early leaders in America who fought for and won the right to include a list of personal liberties in the United States Constitution.

English Bill of Rights of 1689, and on other early legal documents.

The Virginia declaration granted free men the right to a jury trial and freedom from losing their liberty except by the law of the land or the judgment of their peers. A man could not be forced to testify against himself, and he could not be subjected to cruel or unusual punishment.[2] (Women did not have any of these rights at that time.)

Madison and his allies finally won their battle for a list of personal liberties, the Bill of Rights. These ten amendments to the Constitution guarantee citizens a wide range of safeguards, including freedom of religion, speech, and assembly, and protection from illegal search and seizure.

Two of the ten amendments are especially relevant to a discussion of the rights of people accused of crimes. The Fifth Amendment contains a clause whose ideas are similar to those in the Magna Carta: "No person shall . . . be deprived of life, liberty, or property, *without due process of law.*" (Emphasis added.) The Fifth Amendment also protects against self-incrimination— in other words, against people being witnesses against themselves. And the Sixth Amendment says that a person accused of a crime has the right to a "speedy and public" jury trial, a right to be told of the "nature and cause" of the accusation, the right to call witnesses who might support the defense, the right to confront accusers, and the right to have a lawyer to help in the defense.

The Bill of Rights marked an important step toward freedom, but problems remained. In 1833, the United States Supreme Court ruled in *Barron* v. *Baltimore* that the Fifth Amendment's Due Process Clause applied only to actions of the federal government, not to actions of the individual states.[3] The Fifth Amendment—with its guarantees of "life, liberty, or property"—was seen as the basis or foundation of all the other guarantees in the Bill of Rights, or as the vehicle for applying the other amendments. Some people interpreted *Barron* as saying only the federal government had to follow the Bill of Rights, not the individual states. Thus, while the federal government in Washington, D.C., could not deny citizens their right to free speech or a jury trial, state and local officials, in, say, Concord, New Hampshire, or Richmond, Virginia, could pass laws restricting the federal constitutional rights of their citizens.

Soon, a bitter battle emerged over whether the Bill of Rights could be—and should be—imposed on individual states. The most explosive question centered on whether the federal government could force the states to outlaw slavery, since slavery denied African Americans

The original Bill of Rights, (shown here) marked an important step toward freedom for citizens of the United States.

the constitutional guarantees of "life, liberty, or property." The battle between state's rights and the power of the federal government culminated in a bloody national tragedy—the Civil War, which was fought between the Northern Union and the Southern Confederacy from 1861 to 1865.

Thirty-five years after the *Barron* decision, the Due Process Clause was finally applied to individual states. On July 9, 1868, the Fourteenth Amendment to the Constitution was ratified. The amendment said that no *state* could "deprive any person of life, liberty, or property, without due process of law," and that states could not deny their residents "the equal protection of the laws." In other words, states can give equal or more protection than that of the federal government, but states cannot provide less protection.

The Fourteenth Amendment—specifically its Due Process Clause—was aimed at forcing the defeated Confederate states to protect the rights and liberties of former slaves. But the amendment was worded so broadly that eventually it came to affect every aspect of American law. In recent decades, the Due Process Clause has been the centerpiece of landmark rulings aimed at eliminating racism, religious bias, and gender discrimination. Indeed, the Due Process Clause of the Fourteenth Amendment has become what the late

Supreme Court Justice William J. Brennan, Jr., called "the prime tool by which we as citizens are striving to shape a society which truly champions the dignity and worth of the individual as its supreme value."[4]

The Due Process Clause affected how each state operated its individual criminal justice system. Over the decades, the Supreme Court has made it clear that Americans accused of crimes have basic rights that neither the states nor the federal government can take away. For example, the Supreme Court has ruled that police cannot use illegally obtained evidence in criminal trials. In addition, the Supreme Court has upheld the rights of people accused of crimes to have a lawyer, to be told about specific charges against them, to be notified when a court hearing is scheduled, to question their accusers, to call witnesses on their behalf, and not to be forced to testify against themselves.

Not all Americans have enjoyed the same level of protection under the Due Process Clause. While Supreme Court decisions may have spelled out an ideal—or model—of what it means to be fair, social customs or prejudices often delayed putting those ideals into practice. Thus, despite the passage of a national Due Process Clause in the mid-1800s, women were denied the right to vote until 1920 and blacks were forced to attend public schools that were separate from—and usually inferior to—those of whites until 1954.

While juveniles may, at one time, not have enjoyed the same due process rights as adults, many safeguards are in place today. Even so, some aspects of due process and courtroom techniques are different for juveniles than for adults. The origins of the differences between the rights of young people and adults under the United States Constitution and Bill of Rights can be found in the concept of *parens patriae.*

Parens Patriae

In Colonial America, few people paid much attention to whether juveniles had rights. Children were expected to obey their parents and respect their elders. Strict discipline was seen as a benefit to a child's physical and mental well-being.

The colonists adopted a view of raising children that was taken from English common law. In English common law, parents owed their offspring little more than the basic necessities of life and protection from physical harm until they reached adulthood.

The "Body of Liberties" was enacted in 1641 as the first legal code in New England. It made cursing at or striking a parent a crime punishable by death.[5] The Body of Liberties *did* give young people one important safeguard, however. Children could complain to the authorities if a parent abused them.[6] This provision helped set the stage for the government to get involved in the private affairs of a family for the sake of protecting the weak or vulnerable. Over time, the authority of government officials to act on behalf of children evolved into the *parens patriae* doctrine. Like due process, the doctrine of *parens patriae* dates back to ancient English common law and to the idea that the king—the highest symbol of government authority— was the protector and guardian of his subjects.

Despite the tradition of *parens patriae*, however, many children living in America in the eighteenth and nineteenth centuries often received little support or protection from the government. There were few laws to protect children from being forced to work long hours at dangerous jobs in factories and on farms. Juveniles accused of crimes had few rights or protections. Children typically were tried in the same court system used for adults. Judges often had no special understanding or sympathy for young people. If found guilty of a crime, children could be sent to adult prisons where they lived side by side with hardened criminals. The conditions in many of these facilities were so horrible that juries sometimes voted to free a juvenile through a practice known as "jury nullification," even if it was obvious that the child had committed a serious crime.

The failure of the government to shield juveniles from harsh prison conditions came, in part, from the fact that young people had few supporters in those early days. Slowly, however, some Americans began to argue, on moral grounds, that children are not simply miniature adults. They believed that childhood should not be spent in dangerous surroundings, or in the company of adult criminals. The attitude toward children—and children's rights—began to change, especially among intellectuals and religious activists. Children began to be viewed as impressionable beings whose character and future were shaped by their environment and by the opportunities given to them by adults.

In the mid-1800s, religious leaders and social activists—people who wanted to improve the living conditions of the poor and vulnerable—worked to protect the most vulnerable children from abuse and neglect. One pioneer was the Reverend Charles Loring Brace. In 1853, he set up the Children's Aid Society to help New York's homeless and poor children. He described them as a "great multitude of unhappy, deserted, and degraded boys and girls." Reverend Brace was not opposed to child labor. Indeed, he said that the "great temptations" facing the city's less fortunate youth arose from "want of work." Instead, it was his concern about rising vandalism, delinquency, and anarchy in the "dangerous classes," coupled with his sense of Christian mission, that motivated him. "For the most part," he wrote, "the boys grow up utterly by themselves. No one cares for them, and they care for no one. Some live by begging, by petty pilferings, by bold robbery." And girls, the Reverend Brace went on to say,

> traverse the low, vile streets alone. . . . They grow up passionate, ungoverned. . . . These boys and girls . . . will, assuredly, if unreclaimed, poison society all around them. They will help to form the great multitude of robbers, thieves and vagrants who are now such a burden upon the law-respecting community.[7]

Other groups concerned about child poverty and juvenile crime followed in the Reverend Brace's footsteps. For example, the Quakers, a religious group known for humanitarian work, established homes in New York to provide refuge and education to homeless or wayward boys and girls. While the homes gave shelter and food, conditions were harsh and the rules were strict. At the first House of Refuge in New York, children worked an eight-hour day at a trade or craft, and went to school for four hours more.[8]

In the late 1800s, a period known as the Progressive Era began. Social reformers worried about the effects that powerful corporations and big cities were having on the nation's most vulnerable citizens, including children. One of the issues they worried about most was juvenile crime and punishment. While refuge homes and reform schools had helped some, children still were falling into lives of crime and poverty. The criminal justice system seemed unable to deal with the issue. A system specially designed to deal with young people, based on the concept of *parens patriae*, was needed, many reformers believed.

At the turn of the twentieth century, the nation's first juvenile court was established in Chicago. Over the next twenty years, nearly every state would do the same.

The fundamental idea of the juvenile court was that "the state must step in and exercise guardianship over a child found under such adverse social or individual conditions," that crime is the result, according to the Committee of the Chicago Bar Association in 1899. The law proposed

> a plan whereby [a juvenile] may be treated, not as a criminal, or legally charged with a crime, but as a ward of the state, to receive . . . the care, custody, and discipline that are accorded the neglected and dependent child, and which . . . shall approximate . . . that which should be given by its parents.[9]

Despite the law's good intentions, however, the new

juvenile courts often failed to live up to expectations. Judges sometimes went too far in applying the *parens patriae* doctrine. They took children away from their parents and put them in juvenile institutions simply because the parents were too poor or sickly to provide what a court thought was proper care. On the other hand, some juvenile judges missed the point of the new law. Instead of acting like loving, guiding parents, they handed out unreasonably harsh punishment to children, jeopardizing their physical and emotional health.

Juveniles had few ways to protect their rights in such circumstances. Even though the due process doctrine was beginning to take hold as a way for adults to protect their rights in criminal cases, *parens patriae* made it hard for children to assert their constitutional rights in juvenile court proceedings. Because the proceedings were informal and flexible, the juvenile judge could control what happened to a child who was brought before the court. While some judges were compassionate and helpful, many were not. One legal historian went so far as to compare juvenile courts of the early twentieth century to the brutal system of punishment used in medieval England. "The powers of the Star Chamber were a trifle in comparison with those of our juvenile courts," wrote the late Roscoe Pound, a famous legal expert and professor at Harvard Law School.[10]

The United States Constitution contained protections for the rights of adults. But, juvenile courts sometimes made it difficult for young people to protect their constitutional rights.

The *parens patriae* doctrine also took away the power of parents to control the lives of their children as they saw fit. Sometimes the government intruded into what parents regarded as private family matters. The United States Supreme Court acted in the 1920s to limit the power of government to intrude into the private lives of citizens, including parents. In 1923, in *Meyer* v. *Nebraska,* the Court struck down a state school curriculum law that was seen as a violation of the personal liberty of parents and others under the Fourteenth Amendment.[11] Two years later, in *Pierce* v. *Society of Sisters,* the Court invalidated an Oregon law that required children to attend public schools rather than private or religious ones.[12] Both rulings stressed the rights of parents to direct the upbringing of their children and to make decisions as they saw fit. Some legal scholars also believe the decisions reflected the Court's support for children's rights.

But neither ruling dealt directly with the question of whether children accused of crimes should have the same due process rights that were available to adults. As time went on, many critics began to believe that, in the interest of providing a flexible system designed to meet the needs of children, the juvenile court system actually took away young people's constitutional rights to a fair hearing and undermined their liberty as American citizens.

It would be many decades before the doctrine of *parens patriae* and the juvenile court system would be challenged in the United States Supreme Court. That challenge would come from a case in Arizona involving Gerald Francis Gault.

3

The Gault Family Seeks Legal Help

After Judge McGhee sentenced Gerald Gault as a juvenile delinquent and sent him to Fort Grant Industrial School, Gerald's upset parents quickly looked for legal help to gain his freedom.

Someone suggested that they talk with Amelia Dietrich Lewis, an experienced lawyer from Sun City, Arizona, who worked with the Arizona affiliate of the American Civil Liberties Union (ACLU). The ACLU is a nationwide organization that defends the constitutional rights of citizens. (Attorney Lewis was not related to Gerald's friend Ronnie Lewis.)

Amelia Lewis was in her early sixties when she agreed to help the Gaults. She had been practicing law

After Gerald Gault was sent to the Fort Grant Industrial School, his parents sought legal help from Amelia Lewis (shown here). Lewis was an experienced lawyer who worked with the Arizona affiliate of the American Civil Liberties Union.

for some forty years and would continue to do so until two years before her death in 1994 at age ninety-one.

Amelia Lewis knew what it was like to be poor and powerless, as many people in rural Arizona were. She had grown up in the Bronx, New York, as the daughter of a seamstress and a men's store-window dresser. In the early 1920s, after studying for several years, she received her law degree from St. Lawrence Law School (now called Brooklyn Law School). After passing the New York bar exam, she became one of the few female lawyers in the nation at that time.

Amelia Lewis practiced law in New York for thirty-three years, part of that time in the city's juvenile justice system. After her husband died in 1957, she moved to Arizona to join one of her three sons, two of whom were lawyers. She quickly made a name for herself as a deputy county attorney, and also as a lawyer in private practice. Some of her clients were Native Americans who were so poor they would pay Lewis with hand-made jewelry or other items instead of in cash.

When the Gaults asked Lewis to help them free Gerald from reform school, she was immediately drawn to the case. She told the Gaults that she believed their son had been held illegally and that his due process rights had been violated. "I had three sons," she would later explain, "and I never wanted them to be treated this way."[1]

But winning Gerald's release would not be easy. In Arizona, a decision by a juvenile court could not be appealed to the next highest court, as is true of an adult court ruling. Judge McGhee's word on Gerald's detention seemed final. Lewis had only one option. She would go directly to the Arizona Supreme Court and ask the justices there to grant a special order on Gerald's behalf called a writ of *habeas corpus*.

Habeas corpus is an English common law term that in Latin means, "you have the body." A writ of *habeas corpus* is a judicial order that tells a public official to come to court to explain the actions taken. If the official cannot show a good reason for the actions taken, the person must be released. The United States Supreme Court has called a writ of *habeas corpus* "the fundamental instrument for safeguarding individual freedom against arbitrary and lawless state action."[2]

In seeking the writ of *habeas corpus*, the Gaults—through Amelia Lewis—were trying to claim for Gerald what they believed were his due process rights under the Fourteenth Amendment to the United States Constitution.

The Gaults would base their argument on the following due process claims: Gerald had been detained by

39

the Gila County authorities and sent to the Fort Grant Industrial School illegally; Judge McGhee had used insufficient evidence to decide that Gerald was delinquent; the rights of Gerald and his parents were violated because the family was not told they could have a lawyer present at Gerald's hearings; they had received no official notice of the hearings as required by Arizona law; no testimony was taken at the hearings; Gerald's parents were not sure whether Gerald was being charged or was being held as a witness against his friend, Ronnie Lewis; and Ora Cook was not present to testify, causing the Gaults to be unsure if, in fact, she was making an accusation against Gerald.

To prepare the *habeas corpus* petition to the Arizona Supreme Court, Amelia Lewis asked Gerald's parents to tell under oath what they knew about the case. She then submitted their statements to the state Supreme Court in hopes of persuading the Justices to order the writ on Gerald's behalf, and secure his release.

On August 3, 1964, the very same day that the Arizona Supreme Court received the statements of the Gaults and their petition, the court acted. Justice Lorna E. Lockwood ordered the Superior Court of Maricopa County, Arizona, to conduct a hearing to collect all of the important facts of the case and then decide on the *habeas corpus* petition. Two weeks later, on August 17, the hearing began in Judge Fred J. Hyder's courtroom.

The Gaults, Officer Flagg, and Judge McGhee answered questions under oath that day. Gerald did not testify. Ora Cook—the woman who had made the complaint against Gerald—was not present. Judge Hyder quizzed the witnesses from time to time, but most of the questions came from Amelia Lewis and her counterpart in the hearing, Assistant Attorney General Philip Haggerty for the state of Arizona.

Throughout the proceedings, Lewis tried persistently to bring out the facts that would support the Gaults' arguments. Judge Hyder did not allow her to ask all the questions she would have liked, however. Sometimes Haggerty objected and the judge ruled the question inappropriate. But the hearing produced compelling evidence to back up the claim that Gerald Gault had been denied his due process rights.

For example, there was the issue concerning the delivery of proper, official notices of the charge against Gerald and of the upcoming hearing. Gerald's mother testified that the only written notice of any kind that she had received was Officer Flagg's short, typewritten note about Gerald's second hearing on June 15. Officer Flagg explained under oath that when Marjorie Gault came to the detention home on the evening of June 8,

41

he "told her why [Gerald] was there, explained the whole thing to her."[3] On the issue of officially informing the family about the upcoming hearing, Judge McGhee stated that he did not believe that Arizona law required written notification for a juvenile proceeding.[4]

There was also the issue of the petition that Officer Flagg filed on June 9 that declared Gerald to be a "delinquent minor." Gerald's mother testified that she never saw it before the day of the *habeas corpus* hearing when Amelia Lewis showed it to her.

A question arose about whether Gerald's mother knew she could hire a lawyer to help in the case against Gerald. Marjorie Gault testified that although she was aware of that right, she was never officially told she had that right.

Gerald's mother also testified that while she knew she could cross-examine witnesses against her son or call witnesses on his behalf, she was never officially told of that right either. With no witnesses to present evidence—and no evidence to challenge—Gerald's "guilt" came down to Judge McGhee's interpretation of words spoken by Gerald. When Amelia Lewis asked Judge McGhee whether any adult witnesses were put under oath or heard to testify against Gerald, the judge replied, "No. It was all, in my mind, done upon the admission of Gerald Gault."[5] When Amelia Lewis asked the judge if he had ever talked to Ora Cook, Gerald's accuser, the judge said no, adding, "I acted entirely upon the statement of the boys."[6]

Gerald, it appeared, was never told that he could remain silent when being questioned by the authorities, and that anything he said could be used against him. But whether Gerald really confessed to making the phone call was a matter of debate.

Indeed, with no written record of the Gaults' appearances in Judge McGhee's court, it was not surprising that there would be conflicting testimony about what Gerald did—or did not—admit to during the two hearings. Officer Flagg and Judge McGhee both testified that at the first hearing on June 9, Gerald admitted to speaking some of the rude words. Gerald's mother said he had never admitted to using the bad language.

When asked about the June 15 hearing, however, Judge McGhee and Officer Flagg remembered it differently. Juge McGhee said Gerald admitted at the hearing to saying some bad words to Ora Cook, but not the more serious words. Officer Flagg agreed with the Gaults that Gerald did not admit to making the rude comments.

If those parts of the hearing were not confusing enough, the testimony became stranger still when it came to questions concerning the basis for Gerald's delinquency charge.

When Amelia Lewis asked Officer Flagg on what basis he charged Gerald was a "delinquent minor," Flagg replied, "On the fact that the phone calls were made, and when they were traced, it went to his [Gerald's] home. And the fact that when I asked him to recite Mrs. Cook's phone number, he recited it like it was his own."[7]

Officer Flagg also was asked under which part of the Arizona Juvenile Code—the section that defines a delinquent child—Gerald had been charged. His reply, "[W]e set no specific charge in it, other than delinquency."[8]

Judge McGhee also seemed to have trouble explaining the basis for his decision in Gerald's case. He seemed to say that Gerald had broken a state law against using dirty language in the presence of a woman or child. Under the state's juvenile code, a young person who breaks the law is delinquent. When Amelia Lewis asked him under what section of the law he had found Gerald to be delinquent, Judge McGhee replied, "I think it amounts to disturbing the peace."[9]

Judge McGhee also said he based his finding of Gerald's delinquency on the part of the juvenile code that refers to a young person "who habitually [regularly] so deports himself as to injure or endanger the morals or health of himself or others."[10] Pressed by Amelia Lewis to explain which immoral matters Gerald had regularly been involved in, Judge McGhee raised the incident in which Gerald had been accused of stealing a baseball glove and lying to the police. But Judge McGhee admitted that no hearing had ever been held on that matter, and that no formal accusation was ever made against Gerald, because there had been a "lack of material foundation" for the allegation.[11]

The *habeas corpus* hearing went into many other details of Gerald's case. By the time it was over, Amelia Lewis's unrelenting questioning of Officer Flagg and Judge McGhee had raised serious doubts about the way the Gaults had been treated by the authorities in Gila County and about the sanction that had been imposed upon Gerald.

Surely, Amelia Lewis and the Gaults believed, the due process guarantees of the Fourteenth Amendment had been denied in their case. The charges on which Gerald had been sent away to live in confinement for six years were vague and unsubstantiated. It seemed that Judge Hyder would have no choice but to overturn Judge McGhee's decision and to release Gerald under a writ of *habeas corpus*. At least that is what Amelia Lewis and the Gaults hoped and believed. But they were wrong. Without comment, Judge Hyder denied the petition for *habeas corpus*.

The ruling was disappointing. But the Gaults and Amelia Lewis were not about to give up. They would next file an appeal with the Arizona Supreme Court on the *habeas corpus* ruling. There was still hope for Gerald, despite the fact that he would be spending his sixteenth birthday at Fort Grant.

4

The Arizona Supreme Court Speaks

In the fall of 1964, Amelia Lewis filed a forty-nine-page opening brief—a summary of arguments—with the Arizona Supreme Court on behalf of the Gaults. Lewis's brief alleged that a long list of mistakes had been made in both Judge McGhee's and Judge Hyder's courts.

Lewis charged, among other things, that Judge McGhee's juvenile court had failed to give the Gaults a fair hearing on the charges against Gerald and to give them proper notice of the hearing; to tell the Gaults of their right to hire a lawyer or, if they could not afford to hire one of their own, to have one appointed for them by the state; to tell the Gaults they could call

IN THE

Supreme Court

OF THE

State of Arizona

IN the Matter of

PAUL L. GAULT and MARJORIE GAULT, father and mother of GERALD FRANCIS GAULT, a minor,

for a Writ of Habaes Corpus.

No. 8549

APPELLANTS' OPENING BRIEF

AMELIA D. LEWIS
Counsel, Northern Chapter,
Arizona Civil Liberties Union
Attorney for Appellants

Received two copies of the within brief this............day of November, 1964.

....

for the Attorney General

Filed in the Supreme Court of Arizona this................day of November, 1964.

....

Clerk

1

In the fall of 1964, Amelia Lewis filed a brief, a summary of arguments, with the Arizona Supreme Court on behalf of the Gaults. A copy of the front page of that brief is shown here.

witnesses; to make Ora Cook available to testify and be cross-examined; and to give the Gaults fair warning about what might happen to Gerald as a result of the hearing.

The brief also said the juvenile court lacked proper and sufficient evidence against Gerald to decide that he was, in fact, delinquent. In addition, Lewis pointed out the lack of a transcript of the hearings in Judge McGhee's court. The brief went on to explain that it was also a mistake that material in Gerald's probation file was kept hidden from his parents. It was also wrong for Gerald to be removed from his parents' custody with no proof that they were unsuitable caretakers.

The brief further stated that a number of mistakes were made in Judge Hyder's court, including a failure to rule that Gerald's case had been handled improperly by Judge McGhee.

For months after the brief was filed with the Arizona Supreme Court, the Gaults and Amelia Lewis waited for the court to consider Gerald's case and to make a ruling. Finally, on November 10, 1965, the answer came.

In a ruling written by Justice Charles C. Bernstein, the Arizona Supreme Court upheld the decision to deny Gerald's *habeas corpus* petition.[1] Gerald would remain at the Fort Grant Industrial School, just as Judge McGhee had originally intended.

It was not surprising that the Arizona Supreme Court turned down the Gaults' petition. Appeals courts, which review the decisions of lower courts, are often unwilling to change a decision that is based on factual findings. One reason is that if a judge or jury hears evidence firsthand, as Judge McGhee did in Gerald's two hearings, the judge or jury is generally in the best position to evaluate the facts and the honesty of the people offering those facts.

Because there was no written record of what happened in Gerald's hearings before Judge McGhee, the *habeas corpus* court under Judge Hyder and the Arizona Supreme Court would have had a hard time disputing Judge McGhee's decision that Gerald was delinquent. While the Arizona Supreme Court could decide whether or not Judge McGhee's legal conclusion of delinquency was proper, the facts leading to that conclusion were harder to dispute.

The court said it agreed with Judge McGhee that Gerald was a "delinquent child." It found "substantial evidence" to support that finding.[2] The court pointed out that under Arizona's juvenile code, "a violation of the law is delinquency."[3] And Judge McGhee had found

Justice Charles C. Bernstein (shown here) wrote the ruling for the Arizona Supreme Court that denied Gerald Gault freedom from the Fort Grant Industrial School.

Gerald in violation of the Arizona law on vulgar or obscene language.

The Arizona court also noted that Gerald's six-month probation period was still in effect when he came before Judge McGhee on the phone charge. Judge McGhee "could have committed Gerald without any further showing of delinquency if he decided Gerald's welfare and the interests of the state" required it, the court said.[4]

In addition, the Arizona Supreme Court said that it was acceptable for Judge McGhee not to have warned the Gaults ahead of time that Gerald might be sent away if he were found to be delinquent. "We know of no such rule," requiring a juvenile judge to issue such a warning, the court said. "Nor does the concept of a fair hearing suggest a need for the rule."[5] Besides, the Justices said the Gaults had already been given fair warning about Gerald's situation when Judge McGhee dealt with him on the wallet-stealing incident in February 1964. At that time, the court pointed out, Judge McGhee had informed the parents that if Gerald came before the court again, he might be committed.[6]

The Justices also rejected the Gaults' argument that they should have the right to appeal Judge McGhee's decision. "[T]here is no right of appeal from a juvenile court order," they declared. The state's superior courts, under whose jurisdiction the juvenile court operated, had "*exclusive original jurisdiction in all proceedings and matters affecting delinquent children.*"[7]

In addition, the court turned aside another of the Gaults' arguments: that Judge McGhee was wrong to send Gerald away because the juvenile court had failed to prove that the Gaults were unfit parents. A child's best interests and the fitness of the parents are not necessarily connected, the court declared. "[T]he child's welfare is the primary consideration before the juvenile court. . . ."[8]

The Arizona Supreme Court ruling rejected nearly all of the Gaults' claims. Interestingly, though, the Supreme Court agreed with the Gaults on one thing—juveniles accused of wrongdoing *do* have due process rights under both the United States and Arizona constitutions. Juveniles deserve "fairness" in judicial proceedings, the court said. "Justice is as good for them as it is for adults."[9] But the Arizona court disagreed that Gerald and his parents had been denied their due process rights. Under the system established in Arizona, and in many other states, for dealing with juvenile wrongdoing, the Gaults had been treated fairly by Judge McGhee and the other Gila County authorities, the Arizona Supreme Court insisted. Contrary to the

Gaults' claims, their constitutional rights had never been violated, the justices asserted.

Hiding "Youthful Errors"

Explaining how the court came to that conclusion, Justice Bernstein went beyond the facts of Gerald's case and tried to show the relationship between due process rights and the philosophy of the juvenile justice system. One key point was that juvenile courts do not try to punish wayward children or label them as criminals. Rather, the courts seek to help young people become good citizens by taking their individual circumstances into consideration, then using a flexible system of justice to decide what is best for each child.

The idea, he suggested, is to get a wayward youth back on track without putting a permanent blot on the young person's record. "[T]he policy of the juvenile law is to hide youthful errors from the full gaze of the public and bury them in the graveyard of the forgotten past," he wrote.[10]

To that end, Justice Bernstein noted that the state's Constitution required that a juvenile hearing take place informally in the judge's chambers, and that the judge's decision should benefit the youngster's welfare as well as the state's interests. As a result of a juvenile court's ruling, he wrote, a child should not be labeled a "criminal," and a decision in a juvenile case should not be called a "conviction." A juvenile court must destroy all records of a case two years after a child's probation or detention ends, unless the youngster is convicted of some offense in the meantime. That way, the child's record is wiped clean, and the child can begin adult life without carrying the stigma of once having been in trouble with the law.

Justice Bernstein acknowledged that some people felt such a system had problems. A "tide of criticism," had been aimed at juvenile court proceedings, largely because of the "informal, non-adversary procedure," used to determine whether a child is delinquent, he wrote. But he defended the system as the best way to help young people.

"The juvenile court stands in the position of protecting parent rather than a prosecutor," he stated. "It is an effort to substitute protection and guidance for punishment. . . . The aim of the court is to provide individualized justice for children." That is why an adversarial high-pressure system like the one used in adult criminal cases is not used in the juvenile justice system, Justice Bernstein wrote. A delinquent boy or girl is not the "enemy of society," but rather the "child of" society, "and their interests coincide."[11]

Still, the fact that judicial proceedings are informal

does not mean that juveniles accused of wrongdoing lose their constitutional rights to due process of law, said Judge Bernstein. The informality of juvenile court proceedings simply lets a judge overlook "technical matters of procedure." The *parens patriae* doctrine "cannot serve as justification for illegal detention."[12] No court should remove a child from parental custody "except for the gravest of reasons."[13]

Yet, in backing due process rights for juveniles, Justice Bernstein and his fellow justices included an important qualifier in their decision. They said that, although juveniles should have due process rights, those rights are not as broad as the rights of adults who are facing criminal charges. The challenge, the court said, is to figure out which parts of the due process doctrine apply in a juvenile hearing.

That point—that children should have due process rights, but not the full range or degree of rights given to adults—made it possible to deny the Gaults' *habeas corpus* appeal. And so, on claim after claim, the Gaults lost in their effort to overturn Judge McGhee's decision and win Gerald's release.

The court held that even though the Gaults did not receive formal written notice of the charges against Gerald, they clearly knew about them. The Gaults also knew about the hearings before Judge McGhee, the

Justices said. "[I]t is clear that they knew the exact nature of the alleged act of delinquency, including the name of [Mrs. Cook], from the day Gerald was detained. . . ." In addition, the court declared that the Gaults "appeared at both juvenile hearings without complaint of inadequate time" for preparation.[14]

The Arizona Supreme Court also rejected the Gaults' complaint that they were never told that they had the following due process rights in Gerald's case: the right to hire a lawyer; the right to subpoena [order an appearance], confront, and cross-examine witnesses; the right to require witnesses to swear to tell the truth before testifying; and the right to be informed ahead of time of the possible consequences if Gerald were found to be delinquent. "Assuming they have these rights," the court said, "it appears from the record that [the Gaults] knew of [them]." They also knew, according to the court, of the possible consequences of a finding of delinquency.[15]

> Mrs. Gault knew the exact nature of the charge against Gerald from the day he was taken to the detention home. She and Gerald appeared at the first hearing without objection. Mr. and Mrs. Gault, together with Gerald, appeared at the second hearing before Judge McGhee without objection. [The Gaults] knew they could have retained counsel, called witnesses and cross-examined Probation Officer Flagg.[16]

On the question of whether the Gaults knew they could hire a lawyer—and whether they should have been told of that right—the Supreme Court's answer was confusing—and yet it was final.

The court acknowledged that there is disagreement about whether a juvenile court must inform a young person of the right to retain a lawyer. The court had ruled in an earlier case that parents of a child involved in a juvenile case "cannot be denied representation" by a lawyer of their choice. However, the court concluded that due process did not extend this right to juveniles.

There may be times when the juvenile court perceives "conflict between the parent and child," the justices admitted. In those cases, they said, the court can appoint a lawyer to represent the young person. But in general, the court claimed, a parent or a probation officer can protect the child's interests in court as well as a lawyer can.[17]

The Supreme Court also ruled that authorities could avoid telling juveniles that they can remain silent and not give evidence against themselves. The point was important because Judge McGhee questioned Gerald about the alleged phone call to Ora Cook without telling him he did not have to answer. The Justices did not say that juveniles are *not* protected against self-incrimination—that they have no right to remain silent when being questioned by authorities. The Justices said, however, that a juvenile court judge does not have to tell them of that privilege. "We think the necessary flexibility for individualized treatment will be enhanced by a rule which does not require the judge" to tell young people of the privilege, the court stated.[18]

As to whether the Gaults should have been able to confront Ora Cook about her charge, the Arizona Justices said such a right depended on the circumstances. Only if Gerald had said he had not made the phone call in the first place would he have been given the right to challenge witnesses, the court said. "We think the relevancy of confrontation only arises where the charges are denied."[19]

The court also suggested that a juvenile judge could rely on some "hearsay" evidence in deciding a case—something that rarely happens in an adult criminal case. Hearsay is testimony given by someone who tells what another person said or what he or she heard another say, not what was personally observed. The Arizona Supreme Court acknowledged that juvenile courts in some states other than Arizona have disagreed with its approach and banned hearsay evidence or held to other "usual rules of evidence."

But the Justices said that a better rule "allows the judge to consider hearsay [even] though the hearing is contested. . . ." Sworn testimony—testimony made under oath—should be required of witnesses who are part of or "officially related" to the juvenile justice system—people such as police and probation officers. The hearsay on which the judge should be able to rely must be the kind on which "reasonable" people are used to depending in "serious affairs," the court added.[20]

Finally, the Arizona Supreme Court denied the Gaults' claim that there should have been a transcript of the proceedings. "The purpose of a transcript, in some instances, is to support an appeal," the court held.

> But there is no right to an appeal. Furthermore, the evidence [brought forward] at a juvenile hearing is of a confidential nature because it is inadmissible in other courts. . . . We think the juvenile court has discretion to order or deny the taking of a transcript.[21]

The Arizona Supreme Court's ruling was a devastating blow to the Gaults. Gerald had now been confined at the Fort Grant Industrial School for about seventeen months. It looked more and more like he would be there until he turned twenty-one.

For the Gaults, the situation was growing desperate. But Amelia Lewis, their lawyer, was not about to give up. She would appeal to the highest authority in the country—the United States Supreme Court in Washington, D.C.

5

Appealing the Ruling

The Gaults' decision to appeal the ruling of the Arizona Supreme Court brought Gerald's case to the national level. Amelia Lewis and the Arizona affiliate of the American Civil Liberties Union turned to others for help in preparing the mountains of paperwork that would be necessary to argue Gerald's case before the United States Supreme Court's nine Justices.

Amelia Lewis wrote a letter to Norman Dorsen, a college friend of one of her sons and a rising star on the New York legal scene. Dorsen, a law professor at New York University, had been a law clerk for Associate Supreme Court Justice John Marshall Harlan, II, and was on the board of directors of the national ACLU. He would one day become one of the ACLU's chief lawyers and, later, the organization's president. But, for now, he was just the kind of help Amelia Lewis needed.

Though he was only in his thirties at that time, Dorsen had already made a name for himself as an expert on the Fourteenth Amendment and its guarantees of due process and personal liberty. Still, since the issue of juvenile due process was not usually in question, Dorsen did not immediately see the full significance of the Gaults' case. The nation's juvenile courts had been operating pretty much the same way since they were established at the turn of the century, and few juvenile cases had come up for review by higher federal courts.

When Dorsen showed the material on Gerald's case to a friend who was more familiar with juvenile justice issues, she declared, "This is important!" Soon thereafter, Dorsen began writing an appeal for the Gaults to the United States Supreme Court. The appeal was sponsored by the national ACLU and was supported by the group's legal director, Melvin L. Wulf. It asked the Supreme Court to review the Arizona Supreme Court's decision in Gerald's case and to make a final judgment on the arguments.

The path to a hearing before the Supreme Court is complex, and the *Gault* case was no exception. As it turned out, the Court already had accepted a different

After the Gaults' decision to appeal the ruling of the Arizona Supreme Court, attorney Amelia Lewis sought the help of Norman Dorsen (shown here). Dorsen had already made a name for himself as an expert on the Fourteenth Amendment and its guarantees of due process and personal liberty.

case that involved general questions of juvenile justice. But on the last day of June 1966, the Court dismissed the other case and accepted the *Gault* case for review. "It was extraordinarily unusual" for the Court to make such a move, said Dorsen some thirty-five years later.[1] Typically the Court would have decided the two cases together, or postponed the newer case until the other one was decided. But the Court seemed to be saying that the facts and circumstances presented by the *Gault* case would allow for a clearer ruling on juvenile rights than those in the other case, according to Dorsen.

The Supreme Court's decision to review the *Gault* case meant that Gerald's lawyers had to get busy. Lengthy legal briefs—summaries of the lawyers' arguments—would need to be written about the constitutional issues presented by the case. Then a lawyer for the Gaults would need to present an oral argument to the Justices of the Supreme Court.

Dorsen had help, primarily from Daniel A. Rezneck, a young Washington lawyer. Rezneck had worked in the law firm of Associate Justice Abe Fortas before Fortas was appointed to the Supreme Court in 1965.

The Gaults' lawyers had one thing on their side. The nation seemed ready for a legal showdown over juvenile justice and due process rights.

Supreme Court Associate Justice Abe Fortas is shown here. Daniel A. Rezneck worked in Fortas's law firm.

In the mid-1960s, juvenile crime was on the rise, and more and more young people found themselves in court. The issue of juvenile court proceedings was on the American public's mind. Many scholars and legal experts wondered whether the old model of juvenile courts, with its flexibility and emphasis on rehabilitation rather than punishment, was still the right one. On the other hand, many supporters felt that with so many young people going before juvenile court judges, it was time to rethink the question of whether children's due process rights were being properly protected under the juvenile court system.

In 1964, about 686,000 cases involving delinquent children, excluding traffic offenses and neglect cases, were heard by the nation's juvenile courts.[2] From 1960 to 1965, arrests for young people under age eighteen rose by 47 percent. In 1965, arrests of people under age eighteen made up one-fifth of the nationwide total for all offenses except traffic violations. In suburban communities, the problem was worse. Youth arrests there represented 32 percent of the total, compared with 19 percent in rural areas.[3]

The rise in juvenile crime and the Supreme Court's interest in due process questions contributed to the importance of the *Gault* case. The circumstances of Gerald's case fit right into a pattern of Fourteenth

Amendment issues that the Supreme Court had been dealing with for a decade.

Earl Warren, a supporter of personal freedom, was Chief Justice of the Supreme Court from 1953 to 1969. Under his leadership, the Court had made a number of landmark decisions that expanded the rights of individuals, especially those who, because they were poor or powerless, were at risk of being abused by the legal system. In cases involving free speech, freedom of religion, racial discrimination, and criminal procedure, the Warren Court put limits on the power of state governments over the lives of citizens. The Court looked for ways to apply the federal protections of the Constitution and Bill of Rights to everyone— including those less fortunate or those whose views were unpopular.

Several decisions by the Warren Court were especially important to the issue of due process rights in adult criminal cases. In 1963, the Court ruled unanimously in *Gideon* v. *Wainwright* that the Due Process Clause of the Fourteenth Amendment requires state courts to provide a lawyer free of charge to people accused of crimes but who are too poor to hire attorneys.[4] The Court overruled an earlier decision that said a lawyer must be appointed for a poor person only in special circumstances, such as mental incapacity. The *Gideon*

Earl Warren, a supporter of personal freedom, was Chief Justice of the Supreme Court from 1953 to 1969.

ruling was important for a number of reasons. It protected the Sixth Amendment guarantee of a lawyer's assistance in a criminal trial. It also showed the Court's concern for the poor and for people who do not have the skill or money to defend themselves against the legal power structure. In addition, it helped extend federal due process rights to the state level.

Interestingly, the lawyer who was appointed to argue Clarence Earl Gideon's case at the Supreme Court level was none other than Abe Fortas, who was then in private practice. When Gerald Gault's case made its way to the Court, Fortas was on the bench and would be one of the Justices deciding Gerald's fate.

Another important decision by the Warren Court came in 1966 in *Miranda* v. *Arizona*.[5] The Court again extended the protections of the Due Process Clause, this time by requiring police to tell criminal suspects of certain constitutional rights before questioning could begin. The decision helped protect people arrested for a crime from self-incrimination, or volunteering information that could be harmful to them and their case. The Court ruled that "prior to any questioning, the person must be warned that he has a right to remain silent, that any statement he does make may be used as evidence against him, and that he has a right to the presence of an attorney."[6]

Several decisions by the Warren Court (shown here) were especially important to the issue of due process rights in adult criminal cases. Front row, from left: Justice John Harlan, Justice Hugo Black, Chief Justice Earl Warren, Justice William Douglas, and Justice William Brennan. Back row, from left: Justice Abe Fortas, Justice Potter Stewart, Justice Byron White, and Justice Thurgood Marshall.

Gideon and Miranda helped lay the groundwork for the Gault case by broadening the reach of due process for people accused of crimes. But both Gideon and Miranda involved adult defendants. Another 1966 decision by the Warren Court had special significance for the juvenile justice system. In Kent v. United States, the Court overturned a juvenile court judge's decision to have a teenage boy tried as an adult for rape and robbery.[7] The judge did not rule on requests from the boy's lawyer to hold a hearing on the question of whether the juvenile court would transfer the case to the adult criminal system, nor would he grant access to the boy's juvenile court records.

Kent was the first case from the juvenile court system to reach the Supreme Court.[8] Many legal observers believe that when the Supreme Court made its decision in Kent, it was ready to address the issue of due process rights for juveniles. But Kent did not present exactly the right set of facts for such a decision. Justice Fortas wrote the majority opinion in Kent. There he hinted at his concerns about the ability of juvenile courts to protect the rights of young people accused of serious crimes.

A child, Justice Fortas wrote, could receive "the worst of both worlds" from juvenile courts—neither the protections given to adults nor the care and rehabilitation envisioned for children.[9] That was a preview of the issues that would arise in Gerald Gault's case when it came before the Supreme Court.

The Arguments

Even though the Supreme Court seemed ready to consider a case involving juvenile due process rights, Gerald Gault's lawyers faced a huge task in preparing an effective argument on behalf of their client. First, they would need to summarize everything that had happened up to that moment in Gerald's case. Then, they would need to present a detailed analysis of past legal cases and social theories to support their claim that Gerald had been treated unjustly. The lawyers would have two chances to persuade the Supreme Court Justices of their claims. First, they would file written material to spell out all of their points (legal briefs). Then, one member of the Gaults' team of lawyers would make oral arguments to the Justices. Opposing lawyers from the state of Arizona, defending the decision of the Arizona Supreme Court, would also have the same opportunities.

Both sides would get support from organizations interested in the issue of due process rights for juveniles. Some of these groups would file written arguments, called *amicus curiae* briefs (friends of the court in Latin). Groups siding with the Gaults included the

National Legal Aid and Defender Association, a Chicago group that supported the rights of poor people in civil and criminal cases; the Legal Aid Society; and the Citizens Committee for Children of New York. The American Parents Committee, a nonprofit association for federal laws on behalf of children, also filed an *amicus* brief.

Siding with the state of Arizona were the Ohio Association of Juvenile Court Judges and the Kansas Association of Probate and Juvenile Judges.

In working on the brief for the Gaults, Daniel Rezneck remembered how he and Dorsen wrestled with how narrowly or how broadly to define the issues in the case.[10] Should the document focus on one or two issues, such as the right to proper notice of charges or the right to cross-examine witnesses? Or should it cover all of the due process issues that were raised by Gerald's encounters with the Gila County authorities?

Even if the Court ruled in favor of the Gaults on only one issue, the lawyers knew it would be enough to overturn the Arizona Supreme Court's ruling. Why risk having the Court dismiss the case or rule against them by making their arguments too broad, complex, and far-reaching? Would it not be better to pick the strongest arguments and argue only those?

On the other hand, each of the due process issues

raised in the case was important. Not only were there questions of proper notice and the right to confront witnesses. There were also the rights to have a lawyer present during the hearing, to be protected against self-incrimination, to have a written transcript of the hearing, and to appeal the juvenile court judge's decision. Presenting all the issues could make the case stronger. If the Gaults lost on some of the issues, they would still have a chance of winning on one or two others. And the chances of that win increased only if all the points were included in the brief.

The lawyers decided to keep all the due process claims in the brief. They hoped to persuade the Supreme Court Justices that the *Gault* case added up to a serious question of individual rights—much like the *Gideon* and *Miranda* cases had. In other words, the Court might see *Gault* as an opportunity to write a landmark opinion on juvenile rights, thus changing the way juvenile courts would operate throughout the nation. "Gault was an invitation to the Court to take a number of criminal-justice doctrines of the '60s and apply them to juvenile law," Mr. Rezneck said.[11]

The lawyers filed an initial statement that addressed the Supreme Court's basis to review the decision of the Arizona Supreme Court. Later, they filed a brief in opposition of the Arizona Supreme Court's decision.

The state of Arizona then filed a brief to counter the Gaults' arguments.

The final step would occur in the chambers of the United States Supreme Court. There Norman Dorsen and Arizona Assistant Attorney General Frank A. Parks would present their oral arguments to the nine Justices.

6

To the United States Supreme Court

It was a big day for Norman Dorsen. He had never presented an oral argument to the United States Supreme Court.[1] Now he would stand before the nine black-robed Justices and try to convince them that they must look beyond the traditional reasoning behind *parens patriae*. He hoped the Justices would see why Gerald Gault's basic rights as a citizen of the United States had been violated by the juvenile court system in Gila County, Arizona.

"I was nervous," Dorsen would recall many years later. But he had prepared carefully for that day. He had written out the long, detailed statement of facts in Gerald's case, and when it was time to stand before the

Norman Dorsen (shown here years after the *Gault* case) recalled that he was nervous when he presented his oral argument on behalf of the Gaults to the United States Supreme Court.

Justices, he spoke clearly, forcefully, and confidently. "This case raises important constitutional questions concerning the extent to which requirements of procedural fairness guaranteed by the due process clause of the Fourteenth Amendment are applicable to juvenile proceedings," he began.[2]

A variety of views were represented on the Supreme Court at that time. Chief Justice Warren probably would not have liked the fact that the case against Gerald involved an alleged obscene phone call. The other Justices on the Court were: Hugo Black, Tom Clark, William Brennan, William Douglas, John Harlan, Potter Stewart, and Byron White.

Norman Dorsen argued that Gerald Gault had been "deprived of his liberty without due process of law." From time to time, one of the Justices would stop him with a question. Some of the Justices seemed skeptical of Dorsen's theories, but others seemed swayed. Justice Tom Clark asked if the Court ruled the way Dorsen wanted, giving a range of due process rights to juveniles, what would be left of the juvenile justice system? "The best part," Dorsen replied. His point was that while due process rights were important in determining the facts of a case and protecting the civil liberties of juveniles, the juvenile court could still exercise its role as a flexible, caring parent in deciding how best to help a young person.

Chief Justice Warren and his fellow Justices continued to listen and ask questions. They too had come prepared for oral arguments. Prior to the session, they had reviewed the detailed legal briefs prepared by lawyers for the Gaults and for the state of Arizona.

The Brief for the Appellants

In the brief for the Gaults, Gerald's parents were identified as the "appellants," because they were appealing the decision of the Arizona Supreme Court. The appellants said the constitutional questions raised by Gerald's case went far beyond what had occurred in Judge McGhee's chambers. Those questions focused on how the "fundamental requirements of procedural fairness," guaranteed by the Due Process Clause of the Fourteenth Amendment, should apply to juvenile court cases.

"Juvenile court proceedings affect thousands of individuals yearly in a way which can adversely determine their future lives," the appellants argued.[3] The *Gault* case was of "substantial importance," because it involved the basic rights of many young people who were being deprived of their liberty without due process of law, according to the appellants.[4] Lawyers for the

Gaults charged that the Arizona Juvenile Criminal Code was unconstitutional. It gave juvenile judges "unlimited discretion" in handling cases but provided no standards to prevent the judges from exercising "arbitrary abuse" over the child.[5]

The appellants also disputed the *parens patriae* doctrine as it applied to the procedure for determining a child's guilt or innocence. It is "no substitute for the fairness that the juvenile is entitled to when his vital interests are at stake," they said.[6] The founders of the juvenile court system wanted judges to look at the individuality of a child, the reasons behind the child's behavior, and the tools the child needed to become a useful citizen.[7] But, the appellants said, "it was a short step from the concept of individualized justice . . . to a greater informality in the trial itself."[8] By trading due process protections for *parens patriae,* the appellants argued, juveniles like Gerald Gault had paid a heavy price. Many safeguards that were common to adult criminal courts had been disregarded by the juvenile courts, leading to a loss of "individual rights," they said.[9] Though the juvenile court movement had "high purposes," those aims were "perverted" by procedures that lacked the basic elements of fairness, according to the appellants.[10]

One by one, the brief touched on what the Gaults

and their lawyers thought were violations of Gerald's basic due process rights:

- Failure to give notice of charges. The appellants argued that citizens accused of crimes should have "a clear understanding" of the charges against them so they could prepare their defense. "Due process requires that a child and his parents be apprised of the charges on which a juvenile is held," they argued.[11] But, they said, the Arizona juvenile code violated that doctrine. It did not give parents and children enough time to prepare for a hearing. The law did require that a petition containing a general charge of delinquency be filed with the juvenile court, the appellants noted. But the young person's parents did not have to be told about the petition.

The Arizona Supreme Court had decided that notice is adequate if the parents are notified of the hearing and told of the facts of the case "no later than the initial hearing by the judge." Only if the charges are denied must the parents be given "reasonable" time to prepare. "This interpretation of adequate notice does not satisfy due process," the appellants declared. If the specific allegations are not given to the child and his parents in a timely manner, they said, "there is no possibility of determining intelligently whether to admit or contest the charges."[12]

- Failure to advise of the right to counsel. The appellants noted that the Arizona Juvenile Code did not provide for the right to counsel—including the right to be told by the judge that parents and a child have a right to hire a lawyer or to be provided one by the state if they cannot hire one themselves. A delinquency hearing has enough "social stigma" and potential for loss of liberty that it is as serious as an adult criminal trial, the appellants argued.[13] Moreover, they said, the wide latitude given to the juvenile court judge by the Arizona Juvenile Code makes effective legal assistance for the child and his parents a matter of "crucial importance."[14]

The appellants also criticized the notion that a juvenile judge—and not a lawyer hired to represent the juvenile—can protect the young person's interests. Such a view, the appellants said, is "unrealistic."[15]

Although a judge may deal with an accused person fairly, they said, the judge cannot investigate the facts of a case, advise and direct the accused person's defense, or participate in confidential conferences.[16]

• Failure to allow confrontation of witnesses. "The child should be able to face the witnesses who give evidence against him, should be permitted to hear such evidence, and should have an opportunity to cross-examine witnesses," they argued.[17] When an accused person denies a legal charge, the only way to test the truth of the accuser's story is by putting it under "the light of cross-examination."[18] This was an opportunity the Gaults never had with Gerald's accuser, Ora Cook.

The appellants also attacked the Arizona Supreme Court's "curious view" that the right to confront witnesses arises only in cases in which a juvenile denies the charges against him. As the appellants point out, Judge McGhee had explained that no adult witnesses were heard and that he did not speak with Ora Cook personally, since he had the "admissions" of Gerald and Ronnie Lewis to go on. The appellants argued,

> This attitude turns topsy-turvy the concept of the juvenile hearing as [a] . . . proceeding to determine the facts based on evidence. It in effect treats the hearing as an inquisition of the accused. . . . The purposes served by the right of confrontation and cross-examination—so important to the proper performance of the court's fact-finding functions—are thereby thwarted.[19]

- Failure to guarantee the privilege against self-incrimination. The appellants pointed to a long line of legal precedents—past legal decisions— that said people could not be forced to testify against themselves, even in noncriminal cases. The Constitution compelled governments to establish guilt through evidence gathered "independently and freely." They "may not by coercion prove a charge against an accused out of his own mouth."[20] And yet, the law in Arizona did not provide for the privilege against self-incrimination in cases involving juveniles.

"It is clear . . . that Gerald Gault ran the risk of self-incrimination when he was questioned at the hearings of June 9 and June 15," the appellants said.[21] Gerald was accused of criminal conduct, and his statements were used as evidence against him. And yet, the appellants said, Gerald was never told that he could remain silent.

- Failure to present the right to appeal and the right to a transcript of the proceedings. The right to appeal a juvenile court decision is of the "utmost importance," argued the appellants. A juvenile code such as the one in Arizona, which gives a juvenile judge "practically unlimited discretion, invites abuse of judicial power if . . .

review by appeal is not provided," the appellants argued. They also argued that "one of the basic shortcomings" of the *Gault* case was the lack of an official record of the proceedings in Judge McGhee's chambers.[22] The appellants pointed out that even if an appeal is not allowed in a juvenile case, the possibility still exists that there will be a *habeas corpus* review, as happened in Gerald's case. "[T]he most elemental notions of due process require that a transcript of the juvenile court proceedings be made, in order to provide an adequate basis for whatever mode of review is deemed appropriate," the appellants concluded.[23]

The Brief for Arizona

The state of Arizona could not have been in greater disagreement with the views of the appellants. In its brief, the Arizona Attorney General's Office, which was the appellee in the case, relied mainly on the reasoning of the state's Supreme Court to defend itself against the Gaults' claims.

Arizona's attorney general "is the first to agree that the child in a juvenile court proceeding is entitled to due process of law," said the state's brief, "but the question . . . is what constitutes due process in such a proceeding."[24]

The state argued that Gerald's due process rights had not been violated even though the normal constitutional safeguards under the Fourteenth Amendment's "fundamental fairness" doctrine were not applied in juvenile courts as they are in adult criminal courts.

Gerald's hearings—two of the 365 hearings held in 1964 before Judge McGhee—were in accordance with the Arizona Juvenile Code, the state's brief stated. The code itself was developed in the same spirit under which the nation's first juvenile courts were created. If due process rules were applied to young people as they are used for adult criminals, the brief noted, the entire juvenile justice system would be "destroyed."[25]

The brief defended the *parens patriae* doctrine as "sound and purposeful" and said that its emphasis on an informal judicial procedure was important for the juvenile justice system to work.

When it came to specifics of the Gaults' due process claims, the Arizona attorney general offered point-by-point responses to the arguments.

- Failure to provide notice of charges and hearing. The state repeated the Arizona Supreme Court's view that the Gaults had received adequate notice of the charges against Gerald and of the upcoming hearings in Judge McGhee's chambers. "Appellants have arrived at the rather curt conclusion that the notice given to Mrs. Gault was non-official," the state's brief said. But notice of the first hearing, on June 9, was given to Mrs. Gault orally by Deputy Probation Officer Flagg, who the brief declared, "was certainly an 'officer' involved in the case."[26] Moreover, the brief states, Officer Flagg told Mrs. Gault why Gerald was being held, and at the June 9 hearing Mrs. Gault was told of the general nature of the charges against her son. Only if Gerald had denied making an obscene phone call would the Gaults have been entitled to more time to prepare a defense, the brief stated.

- Failure to inform of right to counsel. The state's brief suggested it was wrong to compare juvenile court proceedings on this point with those in an adult criminal court. "The philosophy of shielding children from traditional criminal court proceedings . . . is still an admirable approach," the brief argued.[27]

The brief also pointed to disagreement over whether a judge can investigate the facts in a juvenile case, advise the young person, direct his defense, or participate in conferences at which the accused juvenile might want to confess. For one thing, the brief argued, juveniles do not immediately go before the judge. They first pass through an "intake procedure" for the juvenile court. There, the brief said, members of the probation staff could advise the juvenile on the best course of action. "Not only do these professionals make social investigations for the court, but they do counseling as well," said the appellee's brief.[28]

Moreover, the Arizona attorney general contended, few juveniles who go before a juvenile court deny the offense—suggesting that the question of the judge's role as an investigator, adviser, and defender was not all that important.[29]

And finally, if appointment of a lawyer became required, the result in many cases would be that a juvenile court would become "a junior criminal court."

"If the juvenile in every instance is entitled to counsel," the state's brief asked, "who will represent the state? If the local prosecutor must do so, is it not true that the proceeding has acquired all the aspects of an adversary proceeding? [T]his is exactly what must be avoided."[30]

- Failure to inform of right to confront and cross-examine witnesses. The state pointed to testimony from the *habeas corpus* hearing to argue that Gerald admitted that he had made some of the lewd remarks over the phone to

Ora Cook. The state's brief then supported the Arizona Supreme Court's contention that the issue of confronting witnesses is relevant only in cases where a juvenile denies the charges against him. This circumstance, however, did not apply in Gerald's case, the state argued.

- Failure to inform of privilege against self-incrimination. The state's brief noted that the Arizona Supreme Court did not say juveniles have no privilege against self-incrimination. Rather, it said that the juvenile judge did not have to tell the young person about the privilege. The state said the court's ruling in *Miranda*, in which police must tell an adult criminal suspect of the right to remain silent, should not apply to juvenile cases. "We are not . . . dealing with an 'adversary system of criminal justice' as referred to in *Miranda*," the Arizona brief argued. "We are dealing with a non-criminal proceeding where an effort should be made to have the juvenile talk."[31]

The brief quoted the following on the privilege against self-incrimination from the Advisory Council of Judges of the National Council on Crime and Delinquency: "To establish rapport with the child, it is of course essential that the judge encourage him to talk freely. The court can often create an atmosphere that induces him to talk even if he is initially reluctant."[32]

- Failure to advise of right to appeal and to have a transcript of the juvenile proceedings. The brief relied on the Arizona Supreme Court's reasoning once again, saying that "since there is no right to appeal, and since the evidence [brought forth] at a juvenile hearing is of a confidential nature . . . there is no requirement that a transcript be made."[33]

The lines had been clearly drawn. The Gaults had argued that Gerald Gault's liberty had been unlawfully taken away by a system that gave him few ways to defend himself against charges of criminal misconduct. The state had argued that to apply to juveniles the same due process system used for adults would destroy the flexibility of juvenile courts and their therapeutic approach to helping young people improve their lives. What would the United States Supreme Court Justices think? It would be months before anyone would know.

91

7

The Ruling

On May 15, 1967, nearly three years after Gerald Gault was taken into custody at his home in Globe, Arizona, there was good news. The United States Supreme Court ruled that juveniles who are accused of wrongdoing should have many of the same protections that are required in adult trials under the Bill of Rights. The Gault family's long nightmare was nearing an end.

Based on the facts in the case, the Court ruled that in the hearing phase of a case that could result in a young person's confinement in an institution, juveniles or their parents deserve the following important rights: adequate and timely notice of the charges; notice that they have the right to have a lawyer—appointed by the court if needed; and the right to confront and cross-examine accusers and other witnesses. In addition, juveniles must be given adequate notice that they have the privilege against self-incrimination and the right to remain silent during a hearing.

"[N]either the Fourteenth Amendment nor the Bill of Rights is for adults alone," the Court declared.[1] Under the Constitution, it said, "the condition of being a boy dies not justify a kangaroo court."[2] In other words, a trial that violates proper procedures is no more acceptable to a juvenile than it is to an adult.

The Justices did not rule on two other claims by Gerald and his family—that juvenile cases should allow for appeals and that there should be a transcript of proceedings in juvenile hearings.

Justice Abe Fortas wrote the detailed and strongly worded opinion for the Court. The opinion in *Gault* marked the first sweeping change in juvenile justice since the founding of juvenile courts in 1899. The opinion's impact was huge.

"The landmark decision is expected to require that radical changes be made immediately in most of the nation's 3,000 juvenile courts," reported *The New York Times* in a front-page story about the opinion.[3] Monrad Paulsen, a professor at Columbia University Law School, told the newspaper, "What this case means in its most dramatic terms is that for 68 years we've been putting youngsters into juvenile institutions by procedures which we now learn have been unconstitutional."[4]

Joining Justice Fortas in the opinion were Chief Justice Earl Warren and Justices Brennan, Clark, and Douglas. Two other Justices—Black and White—concurred with the majority opinion. Justice Harlan wrote a separate opinion concurring in part and dissenting in part. Justice Black stated that he agreed with the majority, but said that the ruling in *Gault* "strikes a . . . fatal blow to much that is unique about the juvenile courts."[5] Justice Stewart dissented from the majority.

In the majority opinion, Justice Fortas was careful to note that the decision in *Gault* did not affect the entire relationship between juveniles, courts, and police. Rather, he said, it pertained only to circumstances similar to Gerald's—hearings in which a juvenile is determined to be "delinquent" because of alleged misconduct on his part, and in which there is a possibility that he may be sent to a state institution.

The Court ruled that a juvenile who is charged with delinquency, along with his parents or guardians, must receive written notice of "the specific charge or factual allegations"[6] at the "earliest practicable time" before any hearing occurs to decide whether the charge is true.[7] Notice must be given "sufficiently in advance" of the hearing to allow time to prepare.[8] In addition, the

Court said that before such a delinquency hearing can occur, the juvenile and his parents have to be notified of the juvenile's right to be represented by a lawyer— either one hired by the family of the accused or one appointed by the state. Moreover, the Court said that the privilege against self-incrimination applies to juveniles in delinquency hearings, and the young person must be informed that he or she has the right to remain silent during the hearing.

Finally, the Court held that unless there is a "valid confession" that is enough for a finding of delinquency, then a judgment at the hearing has to be based on the sworn testimony of witnesses who can be confronted and cross-examined by the accused minor.[9]

The Court, however, did not grant juveniles every due process right that adults enjoy. The Justices reserved judgment on several issues—whether, for example, a juvenile court may use hearsay evidence or other testimony that is not usually permitted in adult court proceedings.

The Court did not rule on several other issues either. These included whether juveniles have a right to a jury trial, whether juveniles can claim constitutional protection against unreasonable searches and seizures, and whether juveniles have a right to a lawyer *before* a delinquency hearing is held, and, if so, at what point they could demand an attorney's help.[10]

Despite these and other limitations of the opinion in *Gault*, however, the ruling marked a major change in the way juvenile courts had operated for decades. The Court had cast serious doubt on the traditional interpretation of the *parens patriae* doctrine. The Court questioned, for example, the idea that juvenile court trials are civil, not criminal, in nature, and that judges and probation officers adequately protect young people's rights. Justice Fortas's opinion said the meaning of the *parens patriae* doctrine was "murky."[11] He also argued that reliance on the doctrine helped create a "peculiar" system in which "unbridled discretion" is often "a poor substitute for principle and procedure."[12]

"The absence of procedural rules based upon constitutional principle has not always produced fair, efficient, and effective procedures," he wrote. "Departures from established principles of due process have frequently resulted . . . in arbitrariness."[13]

The majority opinion also suggested that many juvenile court judges were poorly equipped for the task of watching out for the interests of the young people who appeared before them in court. In a footnote, Justice Fortas cited statistics showing that half the juvenile judges in 1964 had no undergraduate degree, a fifth had no college education at all, a fifth were not licensed attorneys, and about 75 percent devoted less than a quarter of their time to juvenile matters.[14]

The most significant part of *Gault* was the fact that juveniles have a right to be represented by a lawyer in delinquency cases. Many of the other aspects of the ruling—such as the ability to cross-examine witnesses and the protection against self-incrimination—would be part of good legal advice. The requirement that juveniles should have a right to a lawyer whenever they might be sent to an institution caught the nation off guard. "Initially," *The New York Times* noted, the right-to-counsel requirement "could cause some paralysis in juvenile courts across the country, which could be followed by a scramble to make lawyers available. Few lawyers are familiar with the procedures of juvenile courts."[15]

Even so, the Fortas opinion said it was important that juveniles have advice and help. Probation officers and judges are not equipped for such duty, the Court said. "Probation officers, in the Arizona scheme, are also arresting officers," as well as witnesses against the juvenile, the Court said. "Nor can the judge represent the child. . . . The juvenile needs the assistance of counsel to cope with problems of law, to make skilled inquiry into the facts, to insist upon regularity of the proceedings, and to ascertain whether he has a defense to prepare and submit it."[16]

In stating that juveniles, like adults, have the privilege against self-incrimination, Justice Fortas acknowledged that there could be differences in technique in how a court went about talking with a young person accused of wrongdoing. For example, the age of the accused and whether his parents are present during questioning, and are competent to help, could affect the relationship between the young person and the court. But, Justice Fortas said, there should be no difference in "principle" between the adult and the juvenile justice system when it comes to this privilege.[17]

Justice Fortas noted that one reason for the privilege against self-incrimination is to prevent government authorities from "overcoming the mind and will" of people who are under investigation.[18] Confessions by children, he stated, need "special caution" to be sure that they are reliable and voluntary.[19] Thus, he suggested, children could be even more prone to persuasion than are adults. "It would indeed be surprising if the privilege against self-incrimination were available to hardened criminals but not to children," Justice Fortas wrote.[20]

Justice Harlan, in a lengthy opinion concurring in part and dissenting in part, said that while Judge

McGhee's decision was wrong and should be reversed, he disagreed with some of the majority's conclusions. He wrote that the following three due process restrictions need to be placed on juvenile courts to guarantee "fundamental fairness" in juvenile proceedings: timely notice of proceedings, notice of the right to counsel, and the right to have a written record of the proceedings in case of review or appeal.[21]

In his dissent, Justice Stewart acknowledged that the juvenile court system had not always lived up to its ideals. But, he said, juvenile proceedings are not criminal trials. The Fortas opinion, he added, "serves to convert a juvenile proceeding into a criminal prosecution. . . . [T]o impose the Court's long catalog of requirements upon juvenile proceedings in every area of the country is to invite a long step backward into the nineteenth century. In that era, there were no juvenile proceedings, and a child was tried in a conventional criminal court with all the trappings of a conventional criminal trial."[22]

To illustrate his point, Justice Stewart recounted the case of a twelve-year-old boy who was tried in New Jersey for a killing. "A jury found him guilty of murder, and he was sentenced to death by hanging," wrote Justice Stewart. "The sentence was executed. It was all

Justice Potter Stewart (shown here) was the only Justice to disagree with the majority in the *Gault* decision issued by the Supreme Court of the United States.

very constitutional."[23] But was it an appropriate sentence for a child?

Justice Stewart conceded that juveniles might be entitled to some due process rights, such as protection against "a brutally coerced [forced] confession."[24] But he added, that does not mean that the privilege against self-incrimination must apply in all situations. Similarly, he wrote, due process requires proper notice of proceedings that affect the relationship between parents and their children. "But it certainly does not follow that notice of a juvenile hearing must be framed with all the technical niceties of a criminal indictment [charge]."[25]

"In any event, there is no reason to deal with issues such as these in the present case," he concluded. "The Supreme Court of Arizona found that the parents of Gerald Gault 'knew of their right to counsel, to subpoena and cross-examine witnesses, of the right to confront the witnesses against Gerald and the possible consequences of a finding of delinquency,'" wrote Justice Stewart.[26]

But Justice Stewart was in the minority. The Supreme Court had issued an opinion that marked a resounding victory for Gerald Gault and juvenile rights.

8

Impact on Future Cases

In the decades since the landmark ruling in *Gault*, the nation's juvenile justice system has gone through dramatic changes. Because of *Gault*, juveniles who are taken into custody for alleged wrongdoing now have a right to fair notice of the charges against them, a right to an attorney, and a right to confront their accusers.

Still, *Gault*'s influence on the juvenile justice system has been limited. The Supreme Court has stopped short of granting young people the full range of constitutional protections that are available to adults who are accused of crimes. At the same time, more and more young people who are involved in serious criminal activities are being taken out of the juvenile justice system—with its flexible procedures under the *parens patriae* doctrine—and are being placed in the adult court system, where due process rights are broader, but potential punishments are far harsher. In 1999, in fact, twenty-four states allowed the death penalty to be sought in crimes committed by juveniles.[1]

The changes that resulted from *Gault* have been gradual and steady. The first major juvenile justice ruling by the Supreme Court after *Gault* came in 1970. The case, *In re Winship*, dealt with the question of how much proof was necessary to determine a twelve-year-old boy's guilt for doing something that, if done by an adult, would have been an act of larceny (taking the property of another person with the intent to steal).[2]

The Court ruled that as a matter of due process, when juveniles are charged with an act that would constitute a crime if committed by an adult, the evidence against them must be proved "beyond a reasonable doubt." The Justices overruled a lower court's decision that a looser standard of proof was enough. In the *Winship* opinion, the Court made a special point of saying that observing a strict standard of proof would not "abandon or displace" the advantages of the juvenile justice process.[3]

A dissent by Warren Burger, who replaced Earl Warren in 1969 as Chief Justice of the Court, foretold a coming change in the Supreme Court's thinking about juvenile rights. Chief Justice Burger thought the

The outside of the Supreme Court building is shown here. The *Gault* decision resulted in slow and steady changes to the juvenile justice system. The first major ruling by the Supreme Court was *In re Winship* in 1970.

Court went too far in *Winship* and had unnecessarily hurt the juvenile justice system. "I dissent from further strait-jacketing of an already overly restricted system," he wrote.

> What the juvenile court system needs is not more but less of the trappings of legal procedure and judicial formalism; the juvenile court system requires breathing room and flexibility in order to survive, if it can survive the repeated assaults from this Court.[4]

To understand the significance of Chief Justice Burger's comments and the future direction of the Court after *Winship*, it is important to know something about the history of that time.

When *Winship* came before the Justices, the makeup of the Supreme Court had changed from that in *Gault*. Chief Justice Earl Warren, who had set the tone for many of the Court's decisions in the 1950s and 1960s, including *Gideon*, *Miranda*, *Kent*, and *Gault*, announced his plan to retire. (It became effective in 1969.) President Lyndon Johnson nominated Justice Fortas to become Chief Justice. But Fortas asked Johnson to withdraw his nomination after it ran into opposition in Congress. Some lawmakers felt that the Warren Court—and Justice Fortas in particular—had granted criminals too many rights. Justice Fortas was also the target of criticism for secretly giving President Johnson advice on policy matters. That was considered wrong because Supreme Court Justices are supposed to maintain their independence from the legislative (Congress) and executive (presidential) branches of government so that they do not lose their objectivity in making decisions that could affect national policy.

In any event, Warren Burger—the Justice who had disagreed with the *Winship* decision—was named to the post by President Richard Nixon, who was elected after President Johnson. Chief Justice Burger was more cautious than his predecessor, Earl Warren, about extending due process rights to juveniles.

His caution became evident when another prominent juvenile justice case, *McKeiver* v. *Pennsylvania* came before the Court in 1971.[5] The case dealt with the question of whether juveniles have a right to trial by a jury. The Sixth Amendment of the Constitution guarantees that "[I]n all criminal prosecutions, the accused shall enjoy the right to a speedy and public trial, by an impartial jury. . . ." But in 1967, when the Court extended criminal due process rights to juveniles in *Gault*, the Sixth Amendment right to a jury trial was not considered to be a part of the Fourteenth Amendment as well.[6] That right was extended to adults accused of crimes in 1968 in *Duncan* v. *Louisiana*.[7] But the question of whether juveniles also had a right to a jury trial remained open until *McKeiver*.

Chief Justice Warren Burger (shown here) was more cautious than his predecessor, Earl Warren, had been about extending due process rights to juveniles.

The Supreme Court, including Chief Justice Burger, held that a jury trial is not constitutionally required for a juvenile court hearings. While states were free to pass laws requiring a jury trial in juvenile cases, the Justices did not order them to do so.

The Supreme Court acknowledged that there were "disappointments," "failures," and "shortcomings," in juvenile justice procedures. But, it said, compelling a jury trial could "remake the proceeding into a fully adversary process," and end the juvenile court system's "informal protective" nature.[8] *Gault* and *Winship* had established a due process standard of "fundamental fairness" in juvenile proceedings, one that emphasized fact-finding procedures, the Court said. "[O]ne cannot say that in our legal system the jury is a necessary component of accurate fact finding."[9] In other words, a court could be fair even without a jury.

In many respects, the decision in *McKeiver* signaled a step back from the strong views that were expressed in *Gault*. In *McKeiver*, the Court seemed to put more emphasis on the flexible nature of the *parens patriae* doctrine than on extending the constitutional rights of young people in juvenile trials.

Putting a juvenile hearing on the same level as a criminal trial ignores "every aspect of fairness, of concern, of sympathy, and of paternal attention that the juvenile court system contemplates," the Supreme Court declared in *McKeiver*.[10] It suggested that it was willing to go only so far in granting due process rights to juveniles.

While McKeiver helped to signify an important difference between juvenile and adult criminal courts, other Supreme Court rulings have made the criminal justice system tougher on juveniles, a trend that has increased in recent years. In the 1979 case *Fare* v. *Michael C.*, a juvenile taken into custody on suspicion of murder asked to have his probation officer present.[11] The police declined to call the probation officer, but told the boy that if he wanted to talk without an attorney present, he could. "If you don't want to, you don't have to," the officer added.[12] The juvenile agreed to talk without a lawyer present and gave the police incriminating information related to the crime. Later, the boy sought to exclude the incriminating information on the ground that his rights had been violated. He claimed that his request to see his probation officer was equal to his Fifth Amendment right to remain silent, just as if he had requested the assistance of an attorney. The Court rejected his argument. It said that a juvenile's request to see his probation officer after being taken into custody on suspicion of murder is not the same as a request to remain silent, nor is it the same as asking for an attorney.

The inside of the Supreme Court of the United States is shown here. In 1979, in *Fare* v. *Michael C*, the Court drew further boundaries around juvenile due process rights.

"The fact that a relationship of trust and cooperation between a probation officer and a juvenile might exist . . . does not indicate that the probation officer is capable of rendering effective legal advice sufficient to protect the juvenile's rights during interrogation by the police, or of providing the other services rendered by a lawyer," the Court said.[13]

In the 1980s and 1990s, the Supreme Court, juvenile judges, and state and federal lawmakers took steps to further limit the rights of juveniles accused of wrongdoing. In 1984, for example, the Supreme Court ruled that laws allowing a juvenile to be detained pending a trial do not violate due process when authorities find that a "serious risk" exists that the juvenile may commit more crimes.[14] In rulings in the late 1980s, the Supreme Court made it clear that people can be executed for crimes committed when they were juveniles. In *Standford* v. *Kentucky*, for example, the Court said that the death penalty can be imposed on convicted killers who are as young as sixteen when they commit their crimes.[15] What's more, the practice of trying juveniles in adult court for serious crimes has increased in recent years. In some places, prosecuting attorneys—those trying to convict accused criminals—are even allowed to send juveniles directly into an adult court without holding a hearing on the matter first.[16]

In other ways, the juvenile courts and the doctrine of *parens patriae* continue to change. For instance, many states have moved away from strict confidentiality rules in juvenile cases by requiring that schools be notified when juveniles are arrested or charged with a crime. A number of places have created juvenile "boot camps," which are facilities that seek to rehabilitate youthful offenders by making them work hard and adhere to military-style discipline. And, some states, concerned about the continuing problem of juvenile delinquency, are letting juvenile or family court judges have jurisdiction not only over young people, but also over their parents.

Meanwhile, juvenile courts throughout the nation continue to struggle with the question of how to balance the needs of vulnerable young people, the demands of society for justice and accountability, and the rights of all citizens to be treated fairly by the government.

Questions for Discussion

1. For more than a century, the nation's juvenile courts have operated separately from adult criminal courts. Juvenile courts were designed to provide flexibility to young people who found themselves in trouble. The idea behind juvenile justice has always been to rehabilitate young offenders rather than punish them. But the trade-off means that juveniles have fewer due process rights than adults. Do you think this is fair? Explain your answer.

2. Some states allow people to be put to death for murders they committed when they were juveniles. Do you think such executions should be legal? Explain your answer.

3. Do you think the police should have to tell a juvenile who is suspected of committing a crime, but not yet in custody, that he or she can remain silent and not answer questions from police? Explain your answer.

4. In some states, the prosecuting attorney—the lawyer who represents the police and the local government—decides whether a juvenile accused of a serious crime should be tried in an adult court. In other places, only a juvenile judge has that power. Which system do you think is better and why?

5. While juveniles are permitted to have a jury trial in several states, most juvenile cases do not involve a jury. What are the advantages and disadvantages of jury trials? What are the advantages and disadvantages of a trial without a jury? Explain your answers.

Chapter Notes

Chapter 1. A Neighbor's Complaint

1. *In re Gault*, 387 U.S. 1, 4 (1967).

2. Arizona Juvenile Code, pp. 8-201–8-239.

3. Affidavits and testimony in the August 17, 1964, *habeas corpus* hearing of Gerald Gault, Superior Court of Arizona, Maricopa County, No. 164769.

4. Petition in the form of affidavit by Marjoric Gault in support of application for writ of *habeas corpus*, August 3, 1964, p. 7.

5. *Habeas corpus* hearing, August 17, 1964, testimony of Marjorie Gault, p. 36.

6. Arizona Criminal Code, p. 13-377.

7. *Habeas corpus* hearing, exhibit 4, "Commitment to the State Industrial School No. 2379," August 17, 1964, p. 81.

Chapter 2. Foundations of Due Process

1. Fourteenth Amendment to the United States Constitution, section 1.

2. Samuel Eliot Morison, *The Oxford History of the American People* (New York: Oxford University Press, 1965), p. 272.

3. *Barron* v. *Baltimore*, 32 U.S. (Pet.) 243, (1833).

4. Bernard Schwartz, ed., *The Fourteenth Amendment* (New York: New York University Press, 1970), p. 1.

5. Joseph M. Hawes, *The Children's Rights Movement* (Boston: Twayne Publishers, 1991), p. 4.

6. Ibid., p. 5.

7. Charles Loring Brace, "The Children's Aid Society," vol. 8, *The Annals of America* (Chicago: The Encyclopedia Britannica, 1968), p. 208.

8. Robert E. Shepard, Jr., "One Hundred Years of Juvenile Justice," *Maryland Bar Journal,* November/December 1997, p. 12.

9. "Some 'Unfinished Business' in the Management of Juvenile Delinquency," *Syracuse Law Review*, vol. 2, (1964), p. 628.

10. "Statement of Arizona Civil Liberties Union," Appellants' opening brief to the Arizona Supreme Court, writ of *habeas corpus* on behalf of the Gaults, November 17, 1964, p. 2.

11. *Meyer* v. *Nebraska*, 262 U.S. 390 (1923).

12. *Pierce* v. *Society of Sisters*, 268 U.S. 510 (1925).

Chapter 3. The Gault Family Seeks Legal Help

1. Author interview with Frank Lewis, March 1999.

2. *Harris* v. *Nelson*, 394 U.S. 286, 291 (1969).

3. *Habeas corpus* hearing, testimony of Officer Flagg, August 17, 1964, p. 44.

4. *Habeas corpus* hearing, testimony of Judge McGhee, August 17, 1964, p. 61.

5. Ibid., p. 65.

6. Ibid., p. 76.

7. *Habeas corpus* hearing, testimony of Officer Flagg, August 17, 1964, p. 50.

8. Ibid., p. 52.

9. *Habeas corpus* hearing, testimony of Judge McGhee, August 17, 1964, p. 61.

10. Juvenile Code of Arizona, sec. 8-201 (6) (d).

11. *Habeas corpus* hearing, testimony of Judge McGhee, August 17, 1964, p. 62.

Chapter 4. The Arizona Supreme Court Speaks

1. Supreme Court of the State of Arizona En Banc, In the Matter of the Application of Paul L. Gault and Marjorie Gault, Father and Mother of Gerald Francis Gault, a Minor, for a Writ of *Habeas Corpus*, 99 Ariz. 181, 407 P. 2d 760 (1965).

2. Ibid., p. 193.

3. Ibid.

4. Ibid.

5. Ibid.

6. Ibid.

7. Ibid., p. 186.

8. Ibid., p. 193.

9. Ibid., p. 189.

10. Ibid., p. 190.

11. Ibid., p. 188.

12. Ibid.

13. Ibid., p. 188.

14. Ibid., p. 185

15. Ibid.

16. Ibid., p. 193.

17. Ibid., p. 191.

18. Ibid.

19. Ibid.

20. Ibid., p. 192.

21. Ibid.

Chapter 5. Appealing the Ruling

1. Author telephone interview with Norman Dorsen, March 5, 1999.

2. Children's Bureau of Statistical Services, *Juvenile Court Statistics-1964* (Washington, D.C.: U.S. Children's Bureau of Statistical Services, 1965), n.p.

3. J. Edgar Hoover, "Crime," *The American People's Encyclopedia* (Chicago: Grolier, 1967), p. 170.

4. *Gideon* v. *Wainwright,* 372 U.S., 335 (1963).

5. *Miranda* v. *Arizona,* 384 U.S. 436 (1966).

6. Ibid.

7. *Kent* v. *United States,* 383 U.S. 541 (1966).

8. Joseph M. Hawes, *The Children's Rights Movement* (Boston: Twayne Publishers, 1991), p. 105.

9. *Kent* v. *United States,* 383 U.S. 541, 556 (1966).

10. Author telephone interview with Daniel Rezneck, December 14, 1998.

11. Author telephone interview with Daniel Rezneck, November 12, 1999.

Chapter 6. To the United States Supreme Court

1. Author telephone interview with Norman Dorsen, March 5, 1999.

2. "Oral Arguments for *In Re Gault,*" © 1996–1998 <http://oyez.nwu.edu> The Oyez Project Northwestern University, (November 24, 1999).

3. Apellants' jurisdictional statement, Supreme Court of the United States, no. 116, pp. 11–12.

4. Ibid., p. 12.

5. Ibid.

6. Brief for appellants in the Supreme Court of the United Sates, no. 116, p. 9.

7. Ibid., p. 15.

8. Ibid.

9. Ibid., p. 16.

10. Ibid., p. 13.

11. Appellants' jurisdictional statement, p. 14.

12. Ibid., p. 15.

13. Ibid., p. 16.

14. Ibid.

15. Appellants' brief, p. 40.

16. *Powell* v. *Alabama,* 287 U.S. 45, 61 (1932).

17. Appellants' jurisdictional statement, p. 17.

18. Apellants' brief, p. 40.

19. Ibid., p. 49.

20. *Malloy* v. *Hogan,* 378 U.S. 1, 8 (1964).

21. Appellants' brief, p. 55.

22. Appellants' jurisdictional statement, p. 18.

23. Appellants' brief, p. 63.

24. Brief for appellee, p. 8.

25. Ibid., p. 12.

26. Ibid., p. 19.

27. Ibid., p. 22.

28. Ibid., p. 23.

29. Ibid., pp. 23–24.

30. Ibid., p. 24.

31. Ibid., p. 28.

32. Ibid., p. 29.

33. Ibid., p. 31.

Chapter 7. The Ruling

1. *In re Gault*, 387 U.S. 1, 13 (1967).

2. Ibid., p. 28.

3. Fred P. Graham, "High Court Rules Adult Code Holds in Juvenile Trials," *The New York Times*, May 16, 1967, p. 1.

4. Sidney E. Zion, "Court Ruling on Juveniles Is Hailed as Ending Unfair Treatment," *The New York Times*, May 17, 1967, p. 31.

5. *In re Gault*, 387 U.S. 60 (1967).

6. Ibid., p. 33.

7. Ibid.

8. Ibid.

9. Ibid., p. 57.

10. Norman Dorsen and Daniel A. Rezneck, "In Re Gault and the Future of Juvenile Law," *The Family Quarterly*, no. 4, 1967, p. 1.

11. *In re Gault*, 387 U.S. 16 (1967).

12. Ibid., p. 17.

13. Ibid., p. 18.

14. Ibid., p. 14.

15. Graham, p. 36.

16. *In re Gault*, 387 U.S. 36 (1967).

17. Ibid., p. 55.

18. Ibid., p. 47.

19. Ibid., p. 45.

20. Ibid., p. 47.

21. Ibid., p. 72.

22. Ibid., p. 79.

23. Ibid., p. 80.

24. Ibid.

25. Ibid., p. 81.

26. Ibid.

Chapter 8. Impact on Future Cases

1. Gerald F. Seib, "Youthful Crimes: Do They Justify Death Penalty?" *The Wall Street Journal,* June 16, 1999, p. A28.

2. *In re Winship*, 397 U.S. 358 (1970).

3. Ibid., p. 367.

4. Ibid., p. 376.

5. *McKeiver* v. *Pennsylvania,* 403 U.S. 528 (1971).

6. Kermit L. Hall, ed., *The Oxford Companion to the Supreme Court of the United States* (New York: Oxford University Press, 1992), pp. 538–539.

7. *Duncan* v. *Louisiana,* 391 U.S. 145 (1968).

8. *McKeiver* v. *Pennsylvania,* 403 U.S. 545 (1971).

9. Ibid., p. 543.

10. Ibid., p. 550.

11. *Fare* v. *Michael C.,* 442 U.S. 707 (1979).

12. Ibid., p. 711.

13. Ibid., p. 722.

14. *Schall* v. *Martin,* 467 U.S. 253 (1984).

15. *Stanford* v. *Kentucky,* 492 U.S. 361 (1989); *Thompson* v. *Oklahoma,* 487 U.S. 815 (1988).

16. Janet E. Ainsworth, "The Court's Effectiveness in Protecting the Rights of Juveniles in Delinquency Cases," *The Future of Children: The Juvenile Court* (Los Altos, Calif.: The David and Lucile Packard Foundation, 1996), p. 68.

Glossary

amicus curiae—A person or organization invited as a "friend of the court" to appear in a legal case. The invited person or group has no direct connection to the case, but does have an interest in the outcome.

brief—A document that contains the facts and legal arguments relating to a case.

civil law—A part of the law that is generally separate from criminal law.

criminal law—A part of the law dealing with crimes against the public. Criminal law includes procedures connected with criminal trials.

cross-examination—The chance to ask questions of a witness who has testified for the opposing side.

delinquent—A juvenile who violates the law.

due process of law—Fairness in criminal legal procedures. The Fifth Amendment to the United States Constitution guarantees that "No person shall . . . be deprived of life, liberty, or property without due process of law." Due process is also implied to be required of the states by the Fourteenth Amendment.

habeas corpus—A Latin phrase that means "you have the body." It is a court order that instructs law enforcement officials who have someone in custody to come to court with that person so that the judge can determine whether the person is being lawfully detained. It protects against illegal imprisonment.

hearsay—Testimony by a witness who communicates what other people have said, not what the witness personally knows to be true.

juvenile court—A special division of the adult court system, first introduced in Illinois in 1899. It deals with youthful offenders, usually people under the age of eighteen, who are charged with crimes, neglected by their parents or guardians, or considered uncontrollable.

Magna Carta—A document signed by King John in 1215. It spelled out laws that limited the authority of the English Crown. The "Great Charter" served as the basis for individual rights in Great Britain and helped guide the American Founding Fathers in developing the United States Constitution.

Miranda **warning**—A rule announced by the United States Supreme Court in *Miranda* v. *Arizona* in 1966. It requires law enforcement officials to tell suspects before arrest or questioning that they have the right to remain silent, to have an attorney, and that anything they say can be used against them in court.

parens patriae—A doctrine that says the government is the ultimate guardian of its citizens, especially minors.

Further Reading

Bartollas, Clemens and Stuart J. Miller. *Juvenile Justice in America.* Upper Saddle River, N.J.: Prentice Hall, 1997.

Clement, Mary. *The Juvenile Justice System: Law and Process.* Woburn, Mass.: Butterworth-Heinemann, 1996.

Kowalski, Kathiann M. *Teen Rights: At Home, At School, Online.* Berkeley Heights, N.J.: Enslow Publishers, Inc., 2000.

Kronenwetter, Michael. *Under 18: Knowing Your Rights.* Hillside, N.J. Enslow Publishers, Inc., 1993.

Internet Addresses

Amnesty International-USA
Children's Human Rights Network
<http://www.amnestyusa.org/children/>

Children's Rights Council
<http://www.gocrc.com>

UNICEF—Voices of Youth, Children's Rights
<http://www.unicef.org/voy/meeting/rig/righome.html>

Index